JENNIFER'S
DIARY

JENNIFER'S DIARY

BBC BOOKS

First published 2003. Copyright © Jo Toye 2003
The moral right of the author has been asserted.
Published by BBC Books, BBC Worldwide Ltd,
Woodlands, 80 Wood Lane
London W12 0TT
Copyright © BBC 2003

Photograph on page 175 by Stuart Wood © BBC

ISBN 0 563 48767 4

Commissioning Editor: Emma Shackleton
Project Editor: Catherine Johnson
Copy-editor: Deborah Savage
Designer: Diane Clouting
Picture Researcher: Camilla Fisher
Production Controller: Belinda Rapley

Set in Bembo
Printed and bound in Great Britain by
Mackays of Chatham

Official Archers Website: www.bbc.co.uk/radio4/archers
for Archers episodes in Real Audio, including an audio archive
of the last seven days. The site also features daily plot synopses,
news, information, a map of Ambridge, quizzes and chat.
Official Fan Club: Archers Addicts 0121 683 1951
Web site:www.archers-addicts.com

CONTENTS

INNOCENCE

Friday 12th July 2002

I've been looking at this empty page for ages, not knowing where to start – it must be years since I wrote anything in longhand!

There's an ancient photo, which Mum must have taken, of me sitting up in bed just after Adam was born, sucking a pencil – typical me, just had a baby and all I can think of is trying to write my (very, at the time!) mixed-up emotions down. These days I'm far more used to thinking straight onto computer – and now Brian's bought me a brand new one, I'll be spending even more time staring at the screen. But the computer's actually why I'm writing this in the first place – before they delivered it, I thought I ought to have a bit of a clear-out of my so-called study, and found this – the diary Lilian gave me last Christmas and in which (shamingly) I hadn't written a word. Time to change all that...

Half the year gone already and so much has happened – though I've had to use the wall planner in the kitchen to jog my memory so this will probably be a bit random.

Can't remember much about 1st January! I daresay it involved a leisurely breakfast followed by a long walk for me and a stint in the lambing shed for Brian after a lovely but very late night at the Masked Ball at Lower Loxley. Brian was on very good form, dancing with everyone – Shula, Elizabeth, Ruth, Julia, Mercedes Goodman, Siobhan Hathaway, Mandy Beesborough – and me of course.

(I have to say any worries I may ever have had on the Mandy Beesborough score have long since vanished. As Alice has pertinently observed, a rear that size is one thing when it's wiggling around on Jennifer Lopez in some New York nightclub; quite another when it's bulging over some poor bay mare's saddle at a hunt meet at The Bull. Mandy's face isn't too bad – with her colouring, you'd expect her to realise the benefits of a decent sunscreen – but it's a pity she forgot about her hands, which look like the hands of a hundred year old. Too much curry combing and riding out in all weathers, I suppose. Wonder if anyone's ever Botoxed their hands? Or collagen injections maybe. Perhaps Lilian's got someone she could recommend.)

Had a lovely birthday on 7th. As well as a gorgeous bracelet, which he'd very sweetly secretly bought in Oxford when he went down for the farming conference, Brian treated me to a few days at a health farm which was heavenly. Even nicer, when I got back he was all over me – said he'd really missed me. Only blip was when Adam rang to wish me happy birthday – said he'd chucked in his job and was going travelling round

Africa. No reason given except that he wanted some time to 'get his head together'. Hope he's OK. Do worry about him. Wish he'd come home.

In mid-Feb we went to Hungary for a few days with Caroline and Oliver – Brian and Oliver were looking into investing in a farming concern over there. So while the men were off looking at potato fields, I was on the loose in Budapest with Caroline! Yes, I know, but in fact we got on very well – it was quite funny really, on the first day we were completely museum-ed out by early afternoon but neither of us wanted to admit it. Finally we dropped the act, gave in to philistinism and went shopping! Highly enjoyable – despite what Brian had tried to tell me, the shops were beautiful, some very covetable stuff.

Had had my doubts about being à deux with Caroline at first, for obvious reasons, but she's very much with Oliver now and really, all that's behind us – and, to be honest, not just Brian and her, but Brian and anyone, I think. It's been over 15 years since that liaison and I honestly believe that if Brian had been going to have another affair – another long-standing affair, I mean – he'd have had one by now. I can remember spending hours, days, weeks going through all my options at the time and, having decided to forgive him, realising that there was an inevitable corollary – that I couldn't spend the rest of my life worrying about it happening again. After all, it's something that's completely beyond my control.

Easy to say, I know, almost impossible to do. But I've had to. Anything else would have driven me mad – and driven him away into the bargain. I'm proud now of the fact that I've pretty much succeeded – well, most of the time. Though I'm not writing Brian off in that area. I'm sure –

what am I saying, I know – he still has his little dalliances, his flirtations – he's a powerfully attractive man and women are just drawn to him – but they're only silly infatuations on his part: they last a few weeks, that's all. Whereas we've been together for 25 years, for heaven's sake. What we have is so solid, I really can't feel threatened. The Jane and Alan Clark of Ambridge, Brian called us the other day – I think he was joking!

Spring this year's a bit of a blank – though I know Brian was working terribly hard. When I think about it, his energy, his vigour – it's one of things that have always made him – and keeps him – so attractive. And this amazing ability of his to take on so much, to be across so many things at the same time.

On the face of it, Hungary was Brian's way of fighting back after Borchester Land took the Estate contract off him, but I think there's more to it than that. I don't know what you'd call it – a low boredom threshold, possibly – though I think the interesting thing with Brian is why he constantly needs a new challenge. If I put it to him he'd give me that quizzical, raised-eyebrow look of indulgent disbelief that says 'I'm humouring you, Jenny' but so many things in life have come so easily to him – inheriting when he was still young, being able to buy Home Farm outright... He hasn't had some of the hardships that, say, Phil and Tony have had to go through – and as a couple we didn't have the struggles of most newly-weds – saving for your own house, that sort of thing. He took on Adam and Debbie, of course, and I know in the beginning Adam didn't make things easy for him, but even he soon folded before the sheer force of Brian's personality.

What's Brian been all his life? The most popular boy in the school. Rich. Well-connected. Handsome. So many gifts, they were almost a burden instead of an advantage. Sometimes you need obstacles in your way, something to spur you on – look at my family! Unhappiness, poverty, ambition – Brian wasn't gifted any of these. No wicked fairy at his christening. So he's had to set his own targets in life and the more demanding the better.

Anyway, all spring, this Hungary thing took a lot of setting up – it's quite a gamble, there's a lot of money involved – and Brian was terribly preoccupied. He spent literally hours on the phone, shut away in his office, then zooming off for meetings – he could be quite short with me sometimes. He flew off to Hungary again at the end of March – Easter time. The idea was to sort things out once and for all, but even on the last day there was a delay in signing something and he had to get a later flight. When he got back I was really quite concerned about him, he looked so tired and drawn. He still kept shooting off to meetings all the time, either to do with Hungary – the bank were hopeless, really dragging their feet, apparently – or Borchester Land. There was one morning when he even spent a couple of hours in bed – absolutely unheard of. I was so worried I wanted to call the doctor, but Brian said Tim had enough problems of his own – he and Siobhan had only quite recently split up. Anyway, Brian seemed to revive quickly enough, I see from the calendar the next thing was he was leaping off to East Anglia to look at packing plants.

Mind you, I was working hard myself throughout the spring – still am! I was about to give a couple of copies of my old 'Ambridge: An English Village' book to the Jubilee jumble when I suddenly had a thought. Why

11

not put together another book for Jubilee year – and instead of concentrating on the past, commemorate present-day Ambridge? A sort of village snapshot, if you like, looking back to how things were, because that's always so fascinating, but also celebrating the vibrancy of village life today. Once I mooted it with people, everyone seemed to think it was a brilliant idea, and before I knew it they were deluging me with ideas, photographs they wanted included – well, you can imagine, in this village! Decided to call it the 'Ambridge Archive' and it's come together really well.

I can still remember Mum's face when she came to see me after I'd had Adam – instead of resting I was trying to note it all down! Think I must have still been high on gas and air!

I suppose it was about mid-May I started thinking what we might do for our anniversary on the 20th – decided on a smallish party at home, just family and friends. I thought after last year – our 25th – Brian wouldn't make a big fuss, but he presented me with a beautiful diamond in an antique (30s) setting, and really got quite sentimental, said he'd known from the start I'd be the perfect wife for him and he hoped he hadn't held me back (?) – from my glittering literary career, I presume! We had the loveliest evening, then the very next day poor Brian had the most awful accident on the farm when a hydraulic hose snapped and hit him in the face. He was terribly brave, resisted all my attempts to get him to Tim or to hospital, but I still think it was foolish of him. Honestly, he was lucky not to lose an eye.

We had miserable weather for the Ambridge Jubilee party on 3rd June, good job we'd already done our village photograph at the Millennium, especially as Brian was still sporting his black eye! New village hall loos opened by Mum to much applause, and of course Mr Pullen was the first to use them! Alice helped with the pony rides and Phoebe had a lovely time with the children's activities, Brian seemed to spend most of the day with her on his shoulders. It's very touching, just lately he seems much more interested in her, seems to want to make more of an effort than he ever did with his own daughters. Pity he's come to it so late.

The best thing about June, though, was Kate, Lucas and Nolly coming to stay. I should have said, how ungrateful! Back in January, Mum had very generously given me, Lilian and Tony £5000 each to spend on ourselves. Tony amazed us all by going out and buying an MG Midget, which he's doing up, Lilian slapped her cheque straight into the hand of some liposuction wizard in Switzerland and I knew immediately what I wanted, too – to see Kate again, and in England this time.

It was wonderful to see them for two whole weeks – and for the rest of the family to see them as well, and see how happy and settled Kate is. We did loads together – showed Lucas a few more of the beauty spots of Borsetshire, and they did things on their own, as well – even took Brian by surprise one day by turning up on spec in Felpersham at some hotel where he'd been having a meeting. They were lucky to catch him, he was only still there because Siobhan Hathaway had nabbed him in conversation – anyway, he was thrilled – whisked them off for tea and Nolly had the most massive ice cream – there's a photo of her with it all over her face, inevitably!

It was Phoebe's birthday while they were over and we had her party here, which was a tiny bit fraught – I don't suppose she quite knows what to think about Kate really, and Hayley's always so prickly when Kate's around. But we had lots of laughs as well. There was one funny moment when we were all sitting around in the kitchen, talking about something – oh, I know, big scandal, it turns out that Siobhan Hathaway's pregnant and Kate and Debbie were speculating about who the father is (not Tim, apparently). Brian, who was miles away, thinking about Hungary probably, had uncorked some wine and he suddenly started pouring it all over the table!

It's only a week since Kate and Lucas left. The house seems very quiet, so I was already feeling pretty flat when I had another blow. My publisher, Alex, had asked me out to dinner and I was so excited, had loads of ideas to discuss with him and so on, when he completely whipped the rug out from under my feet by announcing he was retiring, and couldn't take on any new projects! I was absolutely devastated – I've spent the last six months collecting material and it was all shaping up so well. Brian was terribly sweet and supportive, but I didn't really see what I could do about it, except look for another publisher, and who on earth could I find who'd take it on and turn it round in time for it still to come out in Jubilee year, which was the whole point? Then I bumped into Usha and she suggested that I scrap the book idea and set up an 'Ambridge Archive' website instead. I was a bit panicked, but she offered to help with all the technicalities – she's very involved in her firm's website, apparently – and of course, Alice is very keen. I only mentioned it to Brian in passing and the next thing I knew, he'd been out and not only got me the new computer but booked dinner at Grey Gables tonight with Alice, Debbie and Simon to celebrate – and to cheer us all up, he said, for missing Kate.

Honestly, it's at times like this that I realise what a very lovely life I have. In fact, I'd better get ready – I can see that along with the website, this diary's going to be a real distraction...

Saturday 13th July

Had a super evening last night, even Alice not too teenage. Simon proposed a toast to his and Debbie's 'two-years-two-months' anniversary and though Brian looked a bit sour, even he had to admit when we got home that Simon does seem to make Debbie happy.

Monday 15th July

Bumped into Jill, we must get on with planning the fête (11th August). As ever, she's looking for something a bit different as well as the usual stalls. Told her about an old football game I've come across during my researches – a traditional grudge match between Ambridge and Darrington. Wondered if we could do something similar. The only thing is, it sounds rather violent, heads and windows broken, etc. Jill keen. Said I'd do more research.

Poor Jill fretting about Kenton who's been home 3 months now, broken marriage and baby left behind in Australia and seemingly still no idea of what he's going to do with his life. Tried to console her with example of Kate but with Kenton pushing 44, I can see why she's at the end of her tether.

Wednesday 17th July

Taking photos for website nearly all day. At fête meeting, everyone very keen on the football idea, they want me to write out some rules. As if I haven't got enough to do! Brian pointed out tonight that he hasn't had a hot meal since Grey Gables on Friday and asked if not too much trouble if he could request roast beef and all the trimmings for end of October, when website will be up and running and the beet will be in.

Friday 19th July

Brian says barbecue by the pool is not his idea of a hot meal. As he's now in the thick of harvest and never know when he's coming in, feel continuing salad situation is only partly my fault. Offered proper lunch on Sunday, said he'd be out all day. Debbie said on the combine she hoped, but apparently there's someone he has to see about a Borchester Land meeting next Friday. Typical!

Saturday 20th July

Helped Jill put up posters for the fête; she hopes the football match will prove a big draw. Lots of people signing up. Will be wonderful to have fête again, last year's cancelled because of Foot and Mouth. Some still feeling effects, restocking, etc. Borchester market only reopened in April. Section on website perhaps?

Thursday 25th July

Frantic with website. Usha keeps talking about going 'online' in September, which is when I'd intended the book would be published. Seems a bit ambitious to me,

This was the picture they used on the jacket of my first novel – very youthful! Don't think I'd have got away with it for the jacket of my proposed 'Ambridge Archive' if it had gone ahead in book form.

but that's probably because I don't understand as much as she and Alice do about giga-bytes and mega-rams or whatever they're called.

Saturday 27th July

Alice and I spent the morning teasing Brian about not being able to take it any more. His Borchester Land meeting yesterday turned into dinner at which he got a bit carried away with the port and brandy and had to beg a bed off one of the other directors overnight!

Thursday 8th August

Harvest halted through downpour so Brian took chance to leap off and get spare parts. Gone all afternoon, they hadn't got them at usual place apparently. Frantically baking for fête.

Sunday 11th August

Weather forecast 'fair' for fête and rain held off. Football match (literally) wild success but best bit had to be Eddie's 'Dancing Diggers', a (very) pale imitation of JCBs at Royal. Ravel must have been a blur in his grave at mangling of 'Bolero', whole thing completely surreal.

Monday 12th August

Glorious 12th. Harvest seems to be going fairly well, no more rainy days or breakdowns than we can cope with, anyway. Brian must be confident because he's still planning to go grouse shooting in Scotland next week. Debbie happy to cope on condition that he brings her back a brace!

Thursday 15th August

Spoke – well, wrote – too soon. Disaster today when the combine caught fire. Luckily Jeff, who was driving, not hurt, but Brian and

17

Debbie had a row about it, she says it only happened because Brian had nagged him about being slow, so Jeff skimped on checking that the chaff was properly cleared from the drum and it overheated. Anyway, not only is the combine a write-off, but the fire engines charged right across the field, so any of the crop that wasn't burnt out is completely flattened. Brian at a loss what to do – everyone's combines are working flat out, so it's not as simple as hiring one in, or getting contractors. Poor thing keeps saying he'll have to cancel his shooting. Quite beside himself.

Friday 16th August

Oliver Sterling to the rescue. Though it sounds a mad idea, he's suggested that we get a combine put on a low loader and brought over from Hungary. Lull in harvesting at the moment, so they could release one from the farm we've invested in – they've got one the same make as ours. Brian got on the phone straight away, now the only worry is that as Ian, the English farm manager there, was off on a long weekend, the chap he spoke to may not have appreciated the urgency. Tried to calm Brian down, suggested he had a nice relaxing swim as he'd done all he could, but he insisted on charging over to Felpersham for some reason. He just never stops.

Sunday 18th August

I know Brian wanted me to vote for the Referendum Party but I say hurrah for more co-operation with our European partners. The Hungarian combine arrived at lunchtime and by late afternoon Debbie had finished the wheat on Long Field! There was a bit of a pantomime beforehand when Brian was trying to establish where exactly it was and could only get the driver's mobile's answering service – in German! – but David had the brainwave of getting hold of Siobhan Hathaway (as she speaks German) so she could ring and at least leave a cogent message and get the driver to ring back. Brian seemed a bit hesitant at first, and I know why – when she was getting those translations done for him she was phoning him every five minutes and I get the impression he thinks she's a bit of a pain – but he did contact her in the end, because although she's moved – some flat in Felpersham I gather – she'd pressed her mobile number on him, of course. Anyway, by the time she rang back, Debbie had already spotted the low loader coming down the lane, so it all ended happily. And as I said to Brian, he can go off on his shooting trip with a clear conscience!

Friday 23rd August

Toiling away on my website – as have been all week – when Brian got back. Couldn't believe he'd driven all the way back from Scotland in his tweeds in this muggy weather, silly man. He'd had a good time, though, looked really rested and relaxed, as if he'd had a proper holiday. He brought back three brace of grouse, one for Debbie and Simon as promised, and two for us. Thought I'd give one to Mum and Jack, then had a better idea and decided to invite Nigel and Elizabeth over for dinner on Monday. Nigel loves grouse.

Monday 26th August

Not the most successful dinner party ever. Brian seemed rather tense, perhaps it was a bit much to expect him to be sociable after a day at Think Tank in Birmingham with Alice. Elizabeth seemed on edge, too. Had a word with Nigel about it in the kitchen – he acted a bit daffy, like he does, then blurted out that he worries that she works too hard, they'd had a busy day at Lower Loxley with the Bank Holiday. We talked about the Liberty and Livelihood March, less than a month away now. Shula's organising a coach from the village and there's coaches from Darrington and Netherbourne too. Feelings are really running high, though Jill, bless her, has had to be very diplomatic because though of course she's all for supporting village services, she doesn't really approve of the hunt.

Friday 30th August

A bit worried about Debbie and Simon, she's been spending so little time at home what with harvest, he is good to put up with it. Wish she'd take things a bit easier, she was really snappy with him today. And it always affects what he still calls his 'vacations' – she's busy with lambing over his Christmas holiday, and harvesting all over the summer one.

Sunday 8th September

Shock at church when Janet Fisher announced she's leaving for a job in Southampton! Shula tells me idea is that, in fullness of time, Tim will join her there – he's on a 6-month locum in London at the moment. Very odd the way the Hathaway marriage break-up panned out: Tim was the wronged party, but things seem to have worked out so neatly for him with Janet, whom he'd apparently been besotted with all along. Whereas Siobhan's on her own, pregnant, in some grim flat, I presume. Feel quite sorry for her, after all, I've done it myself, it's tough without a partner there for support. And, also like me, she has never named the father.

Monday 9th September

Can't believe it, Brian's announced he's not going to be coming down on the coach with us for the march! He's only gone and got himself involved in some stupid Borchester Land meeting in London on the Friday, says it's not worth traipsing all the way back and forth to London twice in a weekend. So he's proposing to stay down at the Farmers Club, says there's people he can see on the Saturday, he'll meet up with us for the march and travel back on the coach. I'm very hacked off about it, and told him so. Not only is the march supposed to be a concerted effort for the village, I was really looking forward to us doing something together for a change. So much for solidarity.

Thursday 12th September

To the library to do some research for the website, and met Brenda Tucker, borrowing some Great American Novels. Seems she's thinking of starting the new class Simon's running – 20th Century North American Fiction. Rather envy her, I was tempted to sign up myself, but know what Brian'd say! Told her I was sure she'd enjoy it. I should think Simon's a really charismatic teacher.

Monday 16th September

Mercedes Goodman's annual charity do for the retired donkey home/veterinary clinic she supports near Mijas. Brian pleaded tiredness – any excuse – said to give her his apologies and £20 for a sack of carrots. Hardly the same. Felt rather let down (again!) but when I got in he was asleep with such a beatific smile on his face I had to forgive him. I do sometimes forget just how hard he pushes himself.

Website coming along well. We won't quite be ready for a launch this month, but October should see us up and running.

Friday 20th September

Offered to drive Brian to Hollerton Junction to catch his train to London but he insisted on driving himself. Reminded him he said he'd never leave the car there again after the marque badge was ripped off last time, but he seemed unconcerned.

Alice whining about the new saddle she wants for her birthday: she'll be lucky, when I mentioned it to Brian last week he tried to blind me with spreadsheets and told me to tell her she'd better start saving her allowance instead of spending it on fripperies. Put this to her tonight. She strongly refutes (polite way of putting it) that antiseptic face wash and a couple of CDs are fripperies, insists Holly's allowance is half as much again, Brian and I are tight and out of touch. Now in ferocious sulk. Can see am going to have very jolly time on coach with her on Sunday unless she's snapped out of it.

Saturday 21st September

Village really fired up for tomorrow's march. Lots of people have made posters, or at least mounted the ones cut out of 'Farmers Weekly'. Oliver's barbecue the other week made over £500 for the cause. Hope Brian feels well and truly guilty about not being with us on the coach, though he didn't sound very guilty when he rang. So much for all these meetings, when I asked what he'd been doing he said he'd had a swim in the pool at some swanky hotel!

All right for some, have spent last two days poring over Grandad's diaries for website. Think I might do an 'Ambridge at War' section, also one on the role horses have played in the history of the village: super photo from Shula of Chris and Grace when they first opened their stables in 50s.

Alice's mood much improved. Could have something to do with my suggesting trip to Felpersham this morning where I spent £80 on her in Gap.

INCREDULITY

Monday 23rd September

Too tired when we got back yesterday to write anything and, to be honest, too wound up. Nothing to do with the march – exhausting, yes, but exhilarating – so many people, one common cause – the future of the countryside, however you try to politicise it – both uplifting and sobering at the same time. But the march itself became a bit of a side issue alongside Brian.

He found us all right in Shepherd's Bush, though goodness knows how – the more I think about it, the more of a lunatic plan it was all along – and we did the march together. Then, at the end, when we were all standing round working out how best to get back to the coach, he suddenly came up, white as a sheet, said he'd left his Filofax at the Farmers Club and he'd got to get it back. I couldn't take it in at first, it seemed so trivial after the enormity of everything we'd been marching for, so I must have looked a bit blank, and in the next breath, he was jabbering on about going to fetch it — miles in the other direction, of course — but that he'd meet us at the coach. If I hadn't been so tired I might have thought a bit more quickly and insisted they just post it on, but before I knew what to think he'd disappeared. All the tubes were crammed and inevitably he rang as we reached the coach to say he wouldn't make it and he'd have to take the train again.

It was so embarrassing, having to explain to Oliver and George and everyone that having made all this fuss about him needing a seat on the way back he wouldn't need it after all, and Caroline gave me a bit of a funny look, but what else could I do? To be honest, I think everyone thought he and I had had a row and this Filofax thing was just an excuse. Alice was on the back seat with William and Emma and the young ones so Shula came and sat by me, saying Daniel and Alistair had fallen asleep anyway, but I think it was more out of pity. And I must say I felt pretty pitiable.

Absolutely drained when we got back, the traffic was abysmal out of London, complete log jam of coaches, so he was back before us, managing to be both smug and contrite. Could have swung for him. Does he ever think about things from my point of view? Quite ruined yesterday for me. He's been fussing round all day today trying to make it up to me — ludicrous. I'm just waiting to see what fancy present he'll come up with as a peace offering. Alice knows he's in the doghouse, so she's spent all evening dropping hints the size of Lakey Hill about her saddle. Well, good for her. She might as well capitalise on it.

Wednesday 25th September

What did I say? Usha round about the website, gushing about the fancy new digital camera Brian's bought me to take pictures for it, also the new printer he's insisted on ordering though it's not the slightest bit necessary. I know him so well.

Sunday 29th September

Alice fourteen today. Felt rather emotional, about her growing up, I suppose. Brian, still over-compensating madly, had gone and bought her the new saddle she's been wanting, so she was out on Chandler virtually all day, though she's getting a bit big for him. Kate rang in evening. For her birthday tomorrow Lucas is taking her to a fabulous new restaurant, Lucas's sister is babysitting Nolly. He's had another promotion at work, they seem to think the world of him. Kate still doing her voluntary work at the AIDS project.

Both Kate's babies have had a pretty dramatic and unconventional entry into the world: Nolly was almost born on the Blackberry Line, Phoebe in a tepee at Glastonbury.

Monday 30th September

Kate's birthday, she's twenty-five. Can remember telling Brian I was pregnant with her, and how thrilled he was.

Still on his best behaviour, he was very sweet to Alice all yesterday, and actually asked to speak to Kate on the phone. Has warned me he'll be out at a Borchester Land meeting in Felpersham on Wednesday which may drag on apparently.

Jennifer's Diary

Tuesday 1st October

Whenever I venture out in the village, all anyone wants to talk about is the blessed website, when's it launching, what's on it, what they think should be on it, etc., etc. To be honest, wish I'd never gone along with it, but have to smile sweetly and invite them to the launch (drinks and nibbles here, on the 16th) and no, they won't all have to peer at the computer, we've thought of that, Usha's borrowing a projector from work so everyone can see it on a big screen.

Thursday 3rd October

Brian back very late last night – nearly one in the morning. But still up bright and early today for the agronomist. I couldn't get off, then he woke me up coming to bed and I was awake again by half five. Eyeballs feel like they've been rolled in sand, and now have got to spend all day staring at computer and scanning in pictures of the old smithy. But with half the village on my back it's got to be done.

Friday 4th October

Tony got the sharp edge of my tongue today when he said something flip about me being up and about early just because I was at Bridge Farm by about half eight. I shot back something about often being out at the fishing lake collecting fees before he's had breakfast. Honestly, he still thinks, or likes to think, I have the life of Riley.

Tuesday 8th October

Disastrous dinner party with Pat and Tony, just knew Brian's being saintly couldn't last. He spent the entire meal winding Tony up about potatoes and crowing about the return he's getting having forward-sold his Hungarian ones, which Tony disputes are properly organic anyway. Salt

26

in Tony's wounds as the supermarket have rejected a load of his purely on appearance. Pat and I trying to keep the peace. Finally had to threaten everyone with no pudding to get them to change the subject.

wednesday 9th october

Website launch a week away, so last-minute planning meeting with Usha. Alice very sweetly helping construct links from one page to another and desperate to show it all off to Brian, who was here for once. Think he was secretly quite impressed with everything we've done. Have decided I ought to be grateful to the website really, it's actually a better use of the material than a book would ever have been, and am sure it'll get a wider audience. Feel it's also a lovely thing to do for the village. Interesting – and worthwhile, I hope. And it's always good for me to have a really absorbing project. Better than therapy, as Brian would doubtless say.

Thursday 10th october

12 a.m. Terrible, terrible shock when Debbie arrived this evening in dreadful state, floods of tears about Simon. Apparently she opened his phone bill by accident and found several numbers cropping up over and over again, rang one at random and it was Brenda Tucker's! Absolutely ghastly – unthinkable – but this hasn't come out of nowhere, apparently.

Seems she's been hearing since Brenda started his wretched class that they'd been seen together, but she'd dismissed it, or Simon had, saying of course they'd been out – in a crowd, socialising with students is part of the job, and so on. All of which is true, up to a point. But Debbie seems convinced he and Brenda have been having some sort of affair. Really can't believe it. Why would Simon look at someone like her when he's got Debbie? It's not as though there's that many years between Debbie and Brenda, so it can't be that. And she's so – well, common.

Honestly don't know what to think. Brian's never liked Simon, of course – he'd say that was putting it mildly – but I've always thought he was good for Debbie. She can take herself so seriously sometimes, and being married to someone who has a more, well, casual attitude to things I think has relaxed her. Just hope his casual attitude doesn't include casual sex. Surely not. Please no.

Have put Debbie to bed in her old room, with the Pony Club trophies and Wham! poster she insisted on keeping. Broke my heart to see her in her old bed, but looking so lost.

Too late to think straight. Perhaps we'll all feel a bit more clear-headed in the morning.

Friday 11th October

Dreadful day, Simon has been phoning non-stop, Debbie refusing to talk to him, still utterly convinced he's been unfaithful with Brenda.

Feel so torn. One the one hand, impossible to believe he'd do such a thing – he'd have to be mad; but at same time – dreadful, feel so disloyal to Debbie – if he has – well, should she have seen it coming?

I'm not saying I'm on Simon's side, not at all, but he and I did have a conversation only last week about how hard she works, and he did almost imply that this was to the detriment of their social life, if not their relationship. And I have to say I thought the same myself over the summer – harvest's so difficult, he hardly sees her, and she's no company when she is around. Anyway, last week he was invited to some University party and was hoping to persuade Debbie to go with him. But I know for a fact she spent the evening filling in the forms for the LEAF farm audit and left him to go on his own. Don't know what to think.

As Debbie seemed to have clammed up with me, sent Brian to talk to her – well, he virtually offered, which was good. Much to my amazement, because I expected him to tell her to kick Simon out once and for all, he seems to take the same view as I do – that she's got no real proof. In fact he even suggested he should talk to Simon. I know it's tempting, but Debbie'd go mad if we interfered. Though of course I don't want her to be with someone who's making her unhappy, but I would just love to know the facts.

Simply can't believe it of Simon. One of his students? He'd have to be mad after that harassment thing – not that anything was proven, the girl was clearly a fantasist – but those sort of things stick.

Debbie refusing to leave her room. I suppose we just have to leave her. The only tiny bright spot is how concerned Brian has been, really solicitous – he was almost an hour with her. Lovely of him. The best I've felt about Brian for a fortnight.

Sunday 13th October

Got up about half past three to go to loo and Debbie's light was still on. No sound though – maybe she fell asleep with it on. Wonder if she'd agree to see a doctor. Sleeping tablets might be an idea.

Simon keeps ringing, protesting his innocence, but she won't talk to him. She won't let me tell Mum, either. Feel like cancelling the website launch, it's the last thing I need, but Brian says it's good for me to have something else to think about.

Monday 14th October

Was making sausage rolls for the launch – dull, I know, but we're talking the likes of Joe Grundy here – when Elizabeth called. She's been such a good friend to Debbie, sent her up, thinking it might be easier for Debbie to talk to her than to me or Brian. Don't know the upshot but Debbie must see she's got to see Simon sooner or later. Even Brian thinks she should, but neither of us can persuade her.

Wednesday 16th October

12 a.m. Exhausted but too hyper to go to bed. Website launch went well – Joe Grundy in pole position by the buffet all night, what's new – but most people very complimentary about the site and Alice came in for lots of praise, which pleased her. She's been so worried about Debbie.

But all that eclipsed, really, by sudden visitation from Simon about 5 o'clock, saying Brian and I had been keeping him from Debbie and insisting his phone calls to Brenda were all about her coursework. He then went on to admit Brenda possibly had got a bit of a thing for him and acknowledged somewhat shamefacedly that he got a kick out of it. It was sad really. It's never occurred to me before, but he's a bit of a Peter Pan, or Dorian Grey, even, with these silly girls the portrait in the attic. And he seems so genuinely sorry – I should think so, having realised how much he stands to lose. Anyway, rightly or wrongly, have said I'll try and get Debbie to talk to him. Will probably get shouted at, but I don't think she should just give up on her marriage like this. Deep down I don't think Debbie does either. She's not a quitter.

Thursday 17th October

At supper had long chat with Brian about Debbie. He's been so much more involved over this whole thing than I would have expected – really concerned that Debbie should do the right thing. Of course they've always been close – so close I've even been a bit jealous sometimes! So glad we're together on this.

Friday 18th October

Don't know what was going on at Lower Loxley last night but somehow three pairs of Elizabeth's knickers got hoisted up the flagpole! Some drunken escapade involving Kenton and Nigel (of course), Owen the chef (!), Alistair (!!) and the saintly Chaba (!!!). Elizabeth furious – they weren't even sexy ones but some huge 'fat day' pants like Bridget Jones is wearing when she finally gets off with Daniel Cleaver. First smile I've seen on Debbie's face for a while, anyway, and Brian's relieved she seems to be taking an interest in the farm again. On strength of this, he shot off to Felpersham for a meeting – he's had to put so much on hold with Debbie out of action he's hardly been off the farm.

As Debbie seemed a bit more amenable, spoke to her about Simon. She admitted she doesn't know what to think, has been going round and round in circles, etc. I think she does acknowledge her working hours are hard on him – not that that excuses him, but... well, as I said to her, he's a very attractive man. You can see why these young girls might fall for him – just like Debbie did when he was her tutor. And as I pointed out – and I should know – things like this are the price you pay for having a charming and good-looking husband – it doesn't have to mean the end of the marriage. Debbie said she'd think about it.

Saturday 19th October

Decorating the church for Harvest Festival this afternoon with Jill and Susan. Janet bringing wine and nibbles to help us along! Odd to think this'll be her last harvest service here. Suppose we're allowed to ask what her and Tim's plans are now? Wonder how Siobhan's getting on? Baby must be due soon. Must ask Jill, think Elizabeth still sees her.

Monday 21st October

Debbie still thinking. Simon still phoning.

Wednesday 23rd October

11 p.m. Feel positively exhausted by it all. Simon – ever more desperate – on phone first thing. After much prevaricating, Debbie finally agreed to see him tonight, but wouldn't say what she intended doing. To end it? Or was there still something left? Icily polite when he arrived, then they were closeted in the sitting room a good couple of hours – finally emerged all tears and smiles and she's moving back in at the weekend. The relief!

Brian still out so he doesn't know the good news yet. Am going to have long bath with Floris bubbles Mum got me. Tomorrow am booking facial, have aged about ten years since all this blew up.

Thursday 24th October

First time it's felt like a normal day for ages – pall has lifted. Debbie clearly happy, she's moving back to the flat tomorrow. As had no time yesterday, what with to-ings and fro-ings and the emotion of it all, MUST make my Harvest Supper offering today. Have to use our lamb. Fancied doing a five-spice curry but don't want Joe Grundy blaming me for his gippy tummy like he did after the website launch, so am playing safe. Lamb casserole with pearl barley and herb dumplings – that should gum him up!

Friday 25th October

Even Brian's feeling the strain – he's been wonderful these last couple of weeks. Debbie thinks so too. I think he's looking tired, but he's zoomed off somewhere — says he still has lots of meetings to catch up on. Anyway, am off for my facial today – in fact am having a manicure and pedicure too, think I deserve it.

Pity we have to go to Harvest Supper tonight. I'd give anything for a night in, just Brian and me. It feels like ages since the two of us had an early night together. Must make time for a few of those this winter, before we're too ancient and an early night means just that.

Saturday 26th October

Well, given that last night wasn't quite the evening I wanted, the Harvest Supper went very well. Tons of food, all of it locally grown or reared and all of it delicious. Joe Grundy hogging the buffet again, the concept that you make your selection and remove yourself is quite beyond him. Moaning about how he'd had to pay full whack to get in and how there should have been a pensioners' price. The Grundys aren't raising turkeys this year but Eddie's planning to do Christmas trees, or so Joe informed me. Tom complimented me on my casserole which, from the Sausage

King of Ambridge, is high praise. He's thinking of doing a line in 'Christmas pudding' sausages – little sweet ones, with raisins and spices, to go round the turkey. Hopes Underwoods are going to sell them.

Best thing about the supper, though, was Brian and Tony finally burying the hatchet – in the potato salad. Brian was chomping his way through a vast helping – which nearly choked him when he found out Pat had made it – but he did have the grace to apologise for that awful dinner party when he did nothing but lord it over poor Tony and his silver scurf.

Got home to find Debbie and Simon had left me flowers and chocolates and a card saying, 'Thanks for everything'. Love her so. Just hope they'll be all right now.

REPRIEVE

Monday 28th October

Alice on half term. Happily she's planned herself lots to do, as feel absolutely drained – post Debbie-and-Simon stress, I think, plus the website is getting me down. Everyone full of praise for the website at the launch, but now it's up and running, of course, the carping has begun. Why isn't this, that and the other on it? Would I like some happy snaps of Pat and Derek Fletcher's ruby wedding party, could I mention someone else's boarding kennels, what about Hallowe'ens past and present? Well, fine, what about them? Spent ages last week typing up stuff from Grandad's farming diaries – I thought they were fascinating and rashly supposed everyone else would think so too – instead I've got every village elder with any remaining marbles coming up to me contradicting everything they say. Apparently the name of the chap who organised the salvage operation on the plane that came down in Brookfield's barley in 1952 was Wharburton, not Warburton, or so Mr Pullen informs me. It's hardly my fault if Grandad got it wrong! And as if it matters! Haven't people got anything better to do?

8 p.m. Brian cheered me up a bit about the website, says the complainers are the 'green ink' brigade, I should just ignore them. Do love him, he always knows how to calm me down.

wednesday 30th october

Spent all day on the website, but now Brian's backed me up, am determined not to give in to the whingers. Usha came round to help with a couple of the links that weren't working, told me Ruth's father's died – very suddenly of a heart attack. Ruth's gone up to Prudhoe. Dreadful, he wasn't very old at all, early sixties I think. But there is some good news. As part of their 'new start', Debbie and Simon are hoping to move to Ambridge – to Honeysuckle Cottage, if they can afford it! They're going to see it on Friday. It'd be wonderful – for them, of course, their own place at last – and for me too, to have Debbie in the village. I know I see her every day but it's not the same. She and Brian are often so busy I don't really see her for days on end, she's just a blur in the tractor cab. They're getting on well with the beet, anyhow. Brian still catching up on all the meetings he had to cancel while Debbie was having her crisis.

Brian was so thrilled when Debbie decided she wanted a career in farming.

Friday 1st November

Debbie and Simon seeing Honeysuckle about now... wonder how they're getting on. Brian says I mustn't pressure her.

Big hoohah at Lower Loxley last night, Jill tells me – Elizabeth beside herself with Kenton – again! Somehow during their Hallowe'en extravaganza Kenton's stage blood got spilt on one of their beautiful silk carpets – except it wasn't stage blood, but some concoction he and Kathy had created out of tomato ketchup, Ribena – you name it, the worst things in the world for staining. Get the feeling his days there are numbered.

Sunday 3rd November

Bit of a dreary day. Bert round moaning that the photo of The Bull on the website doesn't show his garden to best advantage. Tried to point out it's intended to be a photo of The Bull, not of Woodbine Cottage, but he wants me to use one he's given me which is basically a photo of his obese cat lolling in front of some vulgar salmon gladioli with the pub barely visible in the corner. And there's a line down the middle of it. I give up.

Brian out for ages this afternoon, talking to Greg about the shoot – first big shoot of the season on Wednesday. Reminds me, must make some of those crab and smoked salmon tarts – they always go down well mid-morning if they're shooting through. Forgot to ask Brian what the plan is for the day, are they starting here with coffee, sloe gin, etc. MUST ASK.

As he seemed in quite a good mood when he got back (unusual after a session with Greg!), thought I'd tackle him about Honeysuckle because, having spoken to Debbie, there's no way she and Simon can afford it unless we help them out. I realise the farm's not exactly coining it at the moment but as I said to Brian, most farm managers like Debbie would expect a house thrown in with the job, so it's almost as if he's exploiting her. Brian says she's paid more than the average manager, blah, blah, but I think he must feel a bit guilty because when I said that we could probably get the Hathaways to knock a bit off – they must be pretty desperate to sell by now – he said he'd think about it. So fingers crossed!

Wednesday 6th November

Shoot seemed to go quite well, or at least my bit, the lunch, did. Rack of lamb with pink peppercorn mash, leeks au gratin, petits pois and asparagus tips, redcurrant and thyme gravy – yes, I know, but it was Matt Crawford and his cronies and Brian seems especially keen to keep on the right side of him at the moment – since all the fuss about the development, I suppose. They wolfed it down, along with some of Brian's best burgundy, didn't get rid of them till nearly six.

Matt cornered me, going on about what a lucky man Brian is to have such a talented and understanding wife. It's true, I can't see Yvette cooking and serving lunch for 12, plus food for the beaters – I should think the kitchen's a bit of a no-go area with those two-inch fake nails of hers – especially when you keep getting messages saying they'll be in at two, no, two-thirty, no, make that make that three-fifteen... Luckily I know by now to add at least an hour to the first time I'm given. Apparently Yvette's taken up riding! It was golf last year – good excuse to tog herself up in Pringle from head to foot, basically – now I suppose she'll be wearing full dressage kit for a hack round the lanes. Alice both sceptical and envious. Yvette's got a 16.2 black mare whereas Alice says her stirrups are practically touching the ground on Chandler these days. But can hardly ask Brian about a new horse for her when I'm still hoping he'll put a chunk towards Honeysuckle.

Thursday 7th November

Success! When he got back from Felpersham this afternoon – assume he'd been to see the bank manager – Brian offered to make up the difference Debbie and Simon need! He wisely suggested offering a bit under the asking price anyway – he's probably right, I'm sure the

Hathaways want a quick sale, and Debbie and Simon are in a good position, first-time buyers, no chain. Debbie absolutely thrilled, so is Alice, so am I. Had to queue to kiss him.

Shoot not quite the unqualified success I'd thought – Matt's friends have complained because Greg made them shoot across the plantation for their last drive, instead of Long Wood. Greg as surly as ever when Brian tackled him about it – how does Helen put up with him? – said the wind had got up, there was no way the birds would have flown high enough. It needles Brian though, Matt's always having a dig of one sort or another.

Cheered him up by telling him about Yvette and the riding. He maintains Yvette is such a classic trophy wife she's bound to run off with her personal trainer before long, then Matt can buy a nice docile Thai bride.

Friday 8th November
Debbie and Simon have put in their offer on Honeysuckle. Fingers crossed.

Sunday 10th November
Remembrance Day service as moving as ever. Doubly poignant with all this talk of 'war on terrorism' and weapons inspectors going into Iraq. World seems such an unstable place.

A bit annoyed when Brian ducked out of coming to the service at the last minute – what he finds to do on a Sunday morning is beyond me, he'd obviously been out in the car because it was parked in a different place when I got back. By this afternoon it was raining so hard he had no excuse (like the famous 'walking the barley', i.e. cruising round in the Range Rover) not to come to tea with Mum and Jack. (I wasn't going to let him get away with 'doing some paperwork' either – i.e. snoozing under the Sunday supplement in the office.) Revenge is so sweet.

Mum looking forward to her birthday on Wednesday and Grey Gables' Nostalgia Night on the 14th. Just hope Jack doesn't try to jitterbug, apparently his dodgy shoulder's only just recovered from the tango at the '30s' dinner dance in the summer.

Monday 11th November

Simon and Debbie's offer's been accepted! The Hathaways didn't even try to haggle – makes you wonder if they could have offered a bit less. Still, they've got it, that's the main thing. It should be straightforward – they could be in by Christmas!

Wednesday 13th November

10 a.m. Just got back from The Lodge. Mum loved her scarf and the Margaret Thatcher book from Debbie and Simon was an inspired idea, except she'll obviously have to fight Jack for it, he was practically snatching it out of her hands. Brian's birthday next week, must chase that tie I've ordered him. The woman seemed a bit vague. Mum and Jack off to Hereford for the day.

11 p.m. Sometimes wish Brian'd talk to me more about the farm. Well, no, I take that back, of course I don't want to know about parasites or NPK or whatever. I mean the big things. Feel sure he's worried about something. Just went into the office when he was playing back his messages and he seemed very on edge. Poured himself a whisky which nearly went all over the desk, then said he wanted a walk. At this time of night!

Hope it's not bad news from Hungary. And he's just committed this money to helping Simon and Debbie. Will try to ask Debbie tactfully if she knows of anything – but don't want her to feel guilty about Honeysuckle and try to back out. Know it's the right move for her and Simon.

Thursday 14th November

12 a.m. Tonight it's me who feels like a stiff drink and a walk to clear my head. Truly bizarre evening, don't know what's going on with Brian.

He knew we were meeting Mum and Jack at seven – I'd reminded him enough times, but he didn't even get in till ten minutes to! Then he had to shower and change and he faffed about so much with his bow tie that I had to do it for him. He'd been out since first thing – God knows what can have been so important in Felpersham that he had to be there that early, or what kept him there all day. No chance to ask him of course – when we got to Grey Gables the music was so loud you couldn't have much of a conversation and it was hardly the time and place. I'm surprised Brian even heard his phone – that the was the next thing, just before we sat down to eat, it rang and he scuttled out to answer it. When he came back he seemed totally spaced out, went through the rest of the evening in a trance. Which was almost a relief – he'd already spilt wine all over me, I dread to think what a mess he'd have made of passing me the gravy.

Don't know what's going on. These evening calls can't be Hungary, they're hours ahead over there surely. Whatever it is, I don't like it.

Friday 15th November

8 a.m. Slept really badly, last evening all whirling round in my head again, then dreamt Brian and I were dancing by the fishing lake and his bow tie was coming undone and he kept saying it was all my fault, I hadn't tied it properly. Or was that a bit of the replay? Well, not the fishing lake bit, obviously. Got up specially to do his breakfast, but he charged out – got to get on with some 'deal' he's involved in. Didn't say when he'd be back.

_3 p.m._ No word from Brian. Asked Debbie if she knew what this deal might be – farm, Borchester Land, whatever, but she hadn't a clue. Had to make light of it so as not to worry her, just when she and Simon are so happy. Made out it was just me being silly and said something flip about male menopause. Though as Debbie observed, it's a bit late for that, he's 59 next week. Must sort out what we're doing – going out? staying in? – and ring that damn woman about his birthday tie, though right now feel I could strangle him with it.

_4 p.m._ Hand-painted tie woman says it's been ready for collection all week – why didn't she phone me then? The way I feel at the moment, certainly don't want to trail all the way to Felpersham to get it, am going to try and get Simon to pick it up for me tonight. Still no word from Brian.

_6 p.m._ Typical, Simon has to chair a meeting this evening as his Head of Department, Sandy, is away. But Debbie says he'll pick it up for me sometime before Wednesday, so that's one less thing to think about. No word from Brian. Am going to feed Alice and Holly, who's staying over, they only want pizza. Was intending duck for Brian and I, not sure what to do.

_7 p.m._ Still no word from Brian. Have had enough. Am going to ring him.

SUSPICION

Saturday 16th November
6.30 a.m. Haven't slept.

Can't get phone call out of my head. Awful, awful, awful. Keep going over what was said – and what wasn't.

Brian didn't sound like himself at all. Really false and strained. Asked when he was coming home, said he wasn't: 'Not now' – whatever that means. Then he said, 'Maybe later – no, tomorrow'. Then he cut me off. Phone then on message service.

Have spent all night trying to talk myself round, calm myself down. It doesn't have to mean anything. But somehow – after the way he's been the last few days – I know it does.

10 p.m. Ghastly, ghastly day. Nearly lunchtime before finally heard Brian's car, had real job composing myself enough even to go downstairs. Just wanted to hide. But couldn't.

Had to face it out.

He was sitting in the kitchen, reading his post and looking all sheepish, of course. Huge bunch of lilies – the ones I don't like, with pink speckled throats like tonsillitis - dumped in sink. Story is his Borchester Land meeting went on, turned into drinks and dinner, wine and port flowing freely, had several too many, couldn't drive, had to stay the night. Well, as stories go, it's not too bad, after all it's happened before – July, I think – but at least that time he was compos mentis enough to make a coherent phone call. But I just know this time it's not true.

Very cool with him. He finally admitted defeat and went to check on deer. Was then out on farm all afternoon. Silent at supper. Now in office 'sorting invoices'.

Very tense. Shoulders in knots.

Sunday 17th November

2 a.m. Can't sleep again. Brian snoring merrily away, could throttle him. To avoid sensational crime of passion, am sitting with feet on Aga and hot milk.

He's got some woman on the go. I know it.

It's absurd. What I mind most is almost not that he's deceiving me again, but the way he's doing it. Why's he being so careless? Don't I deserve a decent story at least?

I knew it, though. Deep, deep, deep down I thought there might be something going on before, after the Countryside March and that business with the Filofax. That whole thing was so bizarre – and that was garbled, too. Completely didn't add up. I even thought about ringing the Farmers Club to see if he really had left it there, but I didn't. Don't ask the questions to which you don't want to know the answers. So I pushed it away.

And then – Debbie and Simon. And that was so dreadful, with her hurting so much, so lost, so betrayed, that, well, it simply eclipsed everything else. I couldn't think about anything apart from Debbie. Except – and this is so awful, I can hardly bring myself to write it, but alongside all the worry for her, the agony I could see she was going through, there was a tiny bit of me thinking - 'well, this is good timing'. If Brian has started one of his little liaisons, I thought, this'll knock it on the head – especially if it's only just begun, especially if it's someone in London. The – what do they call it? – the oxygen of opportunity? – well and truly removed.

And then – with her suffering so and him so caring, it convinced me I must have been imagining it. He was so involved with Debbie, so concerned for her, it underlined what a unit we were, not just me and him, but all of us, the children, a family. Something solid and incontrovertible. And when I said to Debbie about marriages being able to survive affairs, becoming stronger through them, even – I meant it.

What we were going through with her, in fact, was the perfect illustration – Brian and me supporting each other, as well as trying to support her.

And I was so sure I was right. I mean, he was here almost solidly for two whole weeks. Hardly went off the farm – he couldn't with Debbie taken to her bed and then hardly knowing what she was doing. I really thought... But maybe it didn't work like that. Maybe he kept it going on the phone – the farm office, the mobile out in the fields. Plenty of opportunity for that.

So if my first thought was right and it predates Debbie and Simon, it survived the hiatus. Which isn't exactly the best news.

Gone 3 a.m. Must get some sleep, Debbie and Simon are coming to lunch today. Going to spare room.

7 a.m. Have racked my brains trying to remember every single day this month, and what he's been doing. Feel so cross I blindly believed all those rearranged 'meetings' which he'd supposedly postponed during the Debbie thing. Am sure there were some genuine ones, but they did give him a licence to disappear for days on end. And the morning of Remembrance Sunday, even.

I've been so stupid. Talk about denial.

Have been flicking back through diary, of course, looking for clues. Sure there was nothing over the summer, nothing before end of September – if then – so it's not that long-established.

46

She has to be something to do with Borchester Land. Had to stop myself from going into farm office yesterday and finding the minutes of one of their meetings to see if there are any female directors. Wish I could remember what he's told me. So stupid, should have paid more attention.

It doesn't have to be another Board member, of course. Could be the secretary, there must be someone who takes the minutes. But I'm sure Brian said she was some mumsy type, in fact we joked that Yvette had probably vetted her, knowing what Matt's like. Maybe the mumsy one's left. Or was on holiday, and they got in a temp... Or maybe she never was mumsy.

The only woman I can remember him talking about in connection with BL is someone called Cindy. He saw Matt Crawford with her once, according to Matt she was an accountant and he was thinking of bringing her onto the board. An accountant called Cindy? As if, as Alice would say. Don't know what happened about her. I don't see Brian with a Cindy, though, somehow.

It has to be through Borchester Land. Would also explain shenanigans about the coach and the Countryside March – his meeting on the Friday, the staying down on Saturday – but I don't think she's based in London. She's somewhere round here.

This is how it'll be, now – the endless speculation, the way it goes round and round in your head. Dizzying.

What really bothers me is that he's usually so much better at covering his tracks. What was Friday all about? And that late night phone call on

Wednesday, and the way he behaved at Grey Gables? Where'd he been all day? What kind of pressure's she putting him under?

Head splitting. Going to take two more paracetamol.

9 a.m. Have had bath and pulled self together. The only thing I can do is to tighten the leash a bit – have perfect excuse this week with his birthday. If she thinks she's having him that night she's very much mistaken.

11 a.m. Informed Brian have arranged nice family supper here for his birthday Wednesday, said I'd already asked Debbie and Simon (haven't yet, of course). Couldn't resist saying I thought he'd enjoy spending the evening with his 'nearest and dearest'. His face was a picture. Debbie collecting wretched hand-painted silk tie for me today, bringing it over when they come for lunch. He apologised YET AGAIN for Friday night. Managed to needle him that I'd have a word with Matt about increasing tendency for BL meetings to turn into booze-ups. But they're tiny triumphs really. Feel mix of sick and seething.

3 p.m. Debbie and Simon gone, could hardly keep hands off each other while here, obviously couldn't wait to get home and jump into bed – lucky things. Brian managed to wreck the lovely Thomas Pink shirt I bought her – getting her to look at a ewe's feet, it squitted all over her. Ruined. Useful though to have excuse to be in bad mood with him. He is in office hunched over computer. Spreadsheets, supposedly. More probably e-mailing you-know-who.

Simon brought news Siobhan Hathaway has had baby, a boy, Ruairi. At least Elizabeth was with her. Hope she realises what she's taken on.

Attitudes a bit more enlightened than when I had Adam, but she'll still find it a struggle, I bet.

Alice out ice skating, luckily. Am going to lie down for couple of hours.

Monday 18th November

9 a.m. Brian still on best behaviour, asked if there was anything special I wanted for Christmas. (Reminds me, must wrap Adam and Kate's presents, also get into Borchester sometime for that floor puzzle for Nolly.) Felt like saying to him 'A faithful husband, perhaps?' but resisted. Makes me furious just to look at him. Think I might go to Borchester for the day. He can have leftover lamb for lunch – he hates cold lamb.

3 p.m. Didn't feel in mood for spending. Bought a few bits for Phoebe and Nolly. Stupidly went into Underwoods lingerie section to buy Debbie a couple of new bras, couldn't believe dreadful old thing she was wearing on Sunday when she had to change shirt – just stood there absolutely paralysed amongst all the lace and froth, suddenly had vision of Brian undoing bra of some faceless woman. Had to come home.

Brian and I out for a meal – little did I know that at the time he was also wining and dining Caroline all round Borsetshire...

Tuesday 19th November

Brian still grovelling, asked if I wanted to get in extra help for shooting lunch on Thursday as I'll have done major meal for his birthday Wednesday night. Said I'd manage with usual help, thank you very much. Asked me again about Christmas, twinkling about where had I put Tiffany catalogue. He makes me sick. What's he hoping for, a discount for quantity?

Spent day on website. Put in some details about Phil's Carols by Candlelight. Going through motions, really, but it's got to be done.

Wednesday 20th November

Brian's birthday. Phone call early morning, apparently William spent most of last night at police station, having disturbed some poachers. Brian zoomed off to see Greg – genuine I'm sure, he can hardly have set this one up – meant had no time for breakfast, good thing as haven't been able to make self wrap his present, also couldn't bring myself on Monday to choose a card, have dug all-purpose one out of drawer, we can all sign that. Can't bear to look at his tie. When I think of the hours I spent with the woman choosing the design, was so pleased when we came up with pheasants, gun dog and everything – why did I bother? Why should I?

10 p.m. Somewhat forced evening. Brian very late in, has had to have total re-think of shoot with Greg as William has to go to police and give statement tomorrow. Debbie followed me into kitchen, noticing I was a bit quiet, managed to convince her I had headache (true) and was fed up about website (also true) – Derek Fletcher has been going on at me again. She says I should make it a village website, share the load. Can't think about it at the moment. They are having survey on Honeysuckle tomorrow.

Thursday 21st November

9 p.m. Shoot went well, Brian says they always do when Matt Crawford not of the party. Had paid for a 300-bird day, shot through but made good time, in for lunch about half-two. Luckily corporate, so not required to be too much mine hostess, just as well as felt about as welcoming as Lady Macbeth. Find self looking at Brian with utter contempt. Cannot find anything attractive about him at moment.

Can't be bothered to police him this evening, he can be on phone to her all night for all I care. Will let myself off this week, but next week must put on better act. This is not the way to behave. Being harpie at home best way to drive him into her arms.

11 p.m. Can't get off to sleep. Brian still downstairs. Feel very fed up. Such a no-win situation whatever I do. Have to blank it out, like I've done so many times before with these stupid little affairs. And have to believe – it is, it IS – a stupid little affair, not Caroline all over again. Am sure he wouldn't do that again.

Can't confront him. Can't. What would be the point?

11.45 p.m. Still can't sleep. All going round in my head.

In the end, where's the advantage to me in letting on that I know? Even if I did manage to squeeze a confession out of him, what would it achieve? An ugly scene, a row, things said in the heat of the moment...

it's not as if it puts me in any stronger position. It'd only expose my weakness. Because – and I've been through this loop so many times – what, in a situation like this, can I say?

What have I got to offer compared with whatever it is he's getting out of it? We all know what it'll be. She'll be younger, sexier – inevitably more exciting, simply because she's someone new. We've been married 26 years, for God's sake. What else can I possibly offer but more of the same, when obviously the attraction of an affair is precisely that it's something different. Infidelity versus infinity, I suppose.

So I sit it out. How many of these two-bit affairs have I closed my eyes/mind/heart to over the years? They fizzle out. They're about the excitement, the buzz, the challenge, the chase. The feeling young again, the fascination, the temptation, even the guilt. I think he even enjoys the guilt. It's part of the excitement.

No, one more day of wallowing tomorrow, final dose of self-pity, then it's full steam ahead for Christmas. Stir Up Sunday, make the puddings, choose the tree, hang the decorations, fill the freezer, buy the presents, wrap the presents... not pretend it's not happening, but ride over it. Show him everything he's got here – which he knows, he knows - and show him it's worth so much more.

Friday 22nd November

7 p.m. Debbie just rang. She's thrown Simon out. Oh, God. Poor darling, it's so awful. She found him with another woman.

Wanted to go straight over and be with her at the flat, don't want her to be alone, but she wouldn't hear of it. Very cold and calm. Wouldn't say any more.

Can't believe it. Not Brenda, apparently, but who?? What can Simon have been thinking of? What about their reconciliation? The 'new start'? And Honeysuckle? Can't begin to understand – but to think I encouraged her to take him back – almost talked her into it – persuaded by him. Feel quite sick.

Brian went white when I told him. A bit too close to home, perhaps?

Saturday 23rd November

Desperately worried about Debbie. Rang three times this morning before she answered her phone, she insists she's fine, doesn't want to see anyone though. Sounded terrible. Not coming in to work today.

Thank goodness we haven't got a shoot this weekend. Brian had to get Andy in to feed the ewes, grain lorry came whilst Brian was in middle of seeing to the deer, auger playing up, spilt grain in yard. Brian very harassed. Asked me if I'd like to walk crops with him this afternoon, weather has been damp yet not particularly cold, so he's worried about disease, especially if Debbie's going to be off work.

He knows how worried I am about her – we both are. And he's feeling as bad about Simon as I am. I feel I forced them back together, but Brian says he was just the same, convinced at the time reconciliation was right thing. Glad to be talking it through with him, glad he's here. Definite feeling Brian and I are closing ranks against the world. But hate that it's through my poor, poor Debbie.

7 p.m. Debbie's phone on answering machine, also mobile. Wanted to go over but Brian said to leave her. Funny, it was as if he wanted me here – and didn't want to leave me either. Like we are clinging together for support.

Lasagne for supper, Debbie's favourite. Made two, thought I could take her one over tomorrow if she won't come here. Bet she hasn't eaten a thing all weekend.

Sunday 24th November

Went to see Debbie this morning, she was chucking all Simon's stuff into bin bags. Eyes like a panda. She insists she is going for divorce, doesn't want to talk about it. Tried to point out she'll have to, in order to get divorce, don't want her bottling everything up. She did finally tell me who it is – the stupid man's only gone and got involved with his Head of Department's wife!

Brian in yard when I got back. Told him all. Says he could break Simon's neck. It was extraordinary, but maybe he's seen his own situation for what it is – the hurt these things cause. Anyway he gave me a lovely hug and said we'd get Debbie through it, the two of us, we'd all get through it together.

Hardly dare hope. Maybe he'll finish it.

Monday 25th November

Debbie insisted on coming in to work, though she shouldn't have, she looks like a wraith. Brian said she wasn't to go near a tractor, put Andy and Jeff on spraying and hauling silage, left Debbie to concentrate on deer (mindless task) and got her to check supplies for lambing. He had accountant here all day, busy doing forward budgeting.

Wanted Debbie to stay over but she insisted on going back to the flat. I'd promised to go and see Mum tonight, Debbie doesn't want anyone else knowing just yet but said I could tell her Gran. Asked her what was going to happen about Honeysuckle, the survey was fine apparently, she says she doesn't know. Have talked to Brian about it, I don't see why we shouldn't go ahead and buy it for her if that's what she wants. Brian says he would, gladly. He is being marvellous with her.

Fingers crossed on other thing.

Tuesday 26th November

Debbie still like a zombie, obviously not sleeping. She wants me to ring Simon and tell him he can come and collect his stuff from the flat at a time when she's not there. Says she never wants to speak to or see him again. He is lying low, staying with some University chum. As Brian said, hope this chap has locked up his wife and daughters.

Brian has not been off the farm to my knowledge since all this happened. Phone calls are one thing, but surely this affair thing can't last if he doesn't get to see her? Oliver rang, offering Debbie and Brian Smithfield tickets tomorrow, put him off saying they were far too busy.

Alice really upset about Debbie, found her crying this evening. Says she really liked Simon, who can you trust? Who indeed. Said we all felt the same about Simon, we were all taken in by him. Relayed this to Brian. He looked thoughtful.

Jennifer's Diary

Wednesday 27th November

Absolutely chucked it down all day. Brian sent men home, Debbie crashed out upstairs for a couple of hours, probably did her the world of good. Finally sent off Kate's and Adam's parcels, Adam's to Kenya address, he's still travelling but said he would be back there definitely by December. In shop to post them, accosted by Jean Harvey wondering why there wasn't a Christmas section on the website. Don't know who's worse, her or Derek Fletcher, who has put up strings of lights round his hideous Grecian portico, almost as bad as flashing Santa which appeared on Willow Farm roof at weekend as advert for some sort of 'Christmas World' the Grundys are having up there.

Finally steeled self to phone Simon. Pretty strained. He asked if I knew what Debbie was going to do. Just told him to stay well away. Mum says – and she's right – we have to make this the best Christmas we can for Debbie – and her birthday too, can't imagine how awful that's going to be for her. As Mum says, she needs to know there are people around who love her. We all do.

Still amazed at how comprehensively Simon duped us all. Thought I was better judge of character. Mum, however, says she never really trusted him. Never quite believed he liked Sammy as much as he claimed.

Friday 29th November

Elizabeth came round, Debbie must have phoned her. So wish she'd talk to me, but as long as she's talking to someone... when Elizabeth had gone Debbie very sadly told me she'd decided she didn't want to move to Honeysuckle on her own. Doesn't know quite what she does want to do yet, but Honeysuckle had been about her and Simon as a couple – and

56

– this is the worst bit – they were even going to try for a baby.

Can't bear it for her. She has lost everything. So hard to know what to say – not that she'd let me say any of it anyway.

Saturday 30th November

Brian and I spent all last evening talking about Debbie and Simon. I feel so wracked at having promoted Simon's interests, how I helped him get back with her, only for him to hurt her so much. It's as if I connived in deceiving her. Feel I betrayed her as much as Simon did. Brian very sweet, said he'd been just as much to blame, he'd totally bought into the line that Simon was good for Debbie, love of her life, etc. Now wishes he'd horsewhipped him and had him hounded out of Borsetshire.

Still feel he and I are very together in this. Feel very confused. Whilst I suppose he still has plenty of opportunity to see whoever it is, especially in daytime – it's not as if I've got him electronically tagged or am monitoring his mileage or anything – he has definitely been around a bit more. And so lovely when he's here, just feel – well, safer, I suppose. More sure that whatever it is, whoever he's seeing, if he still is, is quite simply insubstantial compared to strength of what we have. And what a bond children are to a couple.

Got to make Christmas cake and puddings today, no time last weekend.

Sunday 1st December

Have had decent couple of nights' sleep at last. Took Phoebe to what Grundys are calling 'Grundy World of Christmas' – mish-mash of craft and other stalls in the Tuckers' yard, Christmas trees and wreaths for sale, plus poor Clarrie and Betty blue with cold, selling cakes, mince pies and teas, and Joe Grundy being Father Christmas in tinsel-bedecked shed. Oh, and Eddie has invented a new line in ornaments – a mooning Father Christmas, delightful.

Debbie in to work, very subdued. Saw Shula and told her about Simon, also called on Jill, but told them to keep it to themselves. Debbie doesn't want whole village gossiping about her.

Monday 2nd December

Christingle service, Phoebe had been picked to light the first Advent candle, she did it so solemnly, bless her. Hayley had done Phoebe's hair in French plait, very pretty.

Debbie arrived late at service, having come from solicitors, they are going to write and get Simon to admit the adultery before petitioning. She's decided she wants to move into what we all still call Kate's cottage. Pleaded with her again to come back to us, but she won't hear of it, says she is 32 (nearly) and can't come running home all the time having meals cooked and getting her washing done (it's never stopped Kenton). Debbie, however, wants a fresh start on her own. Not at all sure this is good idea. She'll only brood, but was told I was fussing so had to shut up.

Wednesday 4th December

Giving cottage a good clean for Debbie – has been empty since the harvest student left – when Lynda Snell appeared, out for a walk. Feared she'd have a complaint about Brian ploughing up a footpath or similar but she started rabbitting on about some party she's having for Hogmanay, would Brian and I go? Tried to flannel we didn't know what we were doing yet. And we don't – Debbie might need us around.

Friday 6th December

Brian had to take Debbie off vaccinating the ewes and send her home mid-afternoon. Then he let off steam to me about how furious he is about all this business with Simon – really do think it's hit home to him. He's been here all day working on DEFRA census figures, has had very little chance to slope off anywhere lately, only to look at that stock trailer the other day – perhaps it's made him think about things, brought them into focus. The farm, the children – there's a whole world here we've built up. Some tawdry affair's not much beside all that.

David came over about Hassett Hills but, as Debbie'd gone home, he and Brian ended up drinking Bourbon in the office, talking about Debbie and Simon I presume. David looked a bit glazed when he stumbled out, said Brian had been saying what a mess everything was.

Saturday 7th December

Helped Debbie move into cottage. She wouldn't let me help unpack. She and Alice went for a long ride. Think it helps both of them.

Monday 9th December

Making pies this evening – apple and mincemeat – for tomorrow's shooting lunch when Debbie announced Simon had been round to see her – God knows how he realised where she was – and told her he's going back to Canada! He says he's given up his job, making out he's being noble so Debbie doesn't have pain of seeing him around, but clearly she thinks (and so do I) he's jumped before he was pushed. He says he can deal with the divorce, which he's not contesting, from there.

Don't know what I think about this. In one sense it's the clean break Debbie wanted, though Brian still says the only clean break that would satisfy him re: Simon, is his neck – not very helpful. But on the other hand, do worry that Simon leaving like this is all too abrupt, that it'll make her think it's all over, done and dusted, and she'll just bury the pain and suffer for it later.

Said to Brian I wished she'd open up more, he says one emotional incontinent (me) in the house is quite enough. But not said nastily.

Tuesday 10th December

Will have to get on to wine merchant tomorrow, Brian has had to buy Matt Crawford off with half a case of his best claret and a bottle of cognac after farcical day's shooting – and after Matt complained last time he was here as well! Don't know what Greg is playing at but he'd forgotten to put a stop on one of the hedges, so the birds got away, then someone's young dog put up a flush of about forty birds at once – so two drives were ruined. Matt very sarcastic, even more so when he discovered a flyer for 'Grundy World of Christmas' stuck on his car.

Wednesday 11th December

Though have tried to make it welcoming for Debbie with Christmas tree, etc., and Mum took round some better curtains, Alice says cottage is squalid and as if Debbie's camping there, so let her take a load of photos down to cheer the place up, one of Adam pulling a face, a family one of us skiing, years ago, and lovely one of Debbie holding Alice as a baby.

Thursday 12th December

So pleased, Elizabeth has persuaded Debbie to go to Lily and Freddie's birthday party this afternoon. As Debbie says, not her usual idea of fun, but at least she'll be among friends, Elizabeth will look after her, and it'll help her forget her troubles for a while.

11 p.m. Brian at a dinner (CLA Christmas shindig, been on wall planner for ages, so I assume bona fide) so tried to write a few more Christmas cards tonight, constantly interrupted by Alice, concerned because Debbie not back from Lower Loxley, no reply from cottage or mobile.

Debbie finally appeared half an hour ago – not sure if the twins' party was such a good idea after all, think putting on brave face may have been too much for her. (Should have realised she might find it too churning, especially as so recently she was hoping for a baby of her own.) Seems she'd been driving around all evening, then got out and gone for a walk, silly girl, her hands were like ice. Have sent Alice to bed, she won't get much sleep this weekend as she's staying at Holly's. Debbie said she wanted to wait up for Brian, something important to discuss with him apparently.

2 a.m. Heard voices downstairs, when I went down Brian and Debbie were still up, both seemed upset. Debbie crying, and saying something about thinking you were the most important person in someone's life when all along you weren't. Brian said he'd said the wrong thing (about Simon, presumably) and upset her. Shooed me back to bed, said he'd make sure she was all right.

Poor, poor love. At least she can talk to Brian. I know she thinks I get too emotional, and with good reason. My poor Debbie. And she's got such a long way to go yet.

REVELATION

Sunday 15th December

5 a.m. Dont' know where to start. Or how. The facts, I suppose.

Brian's been having an affair. Is. With Siobhan Hathaway. He's the father of her baby. He has a son.

Don't know how to go on.

10 a.m. Am in bits.

It's not going to make me feel better – nothing's going to make me feel better, ever – but perhaps it might help me sort things out a bit if I write them down. So I'm just going to write how it happened. How he told me.

Friday morning – the 13th – interesting – woke up very early. Brian not in bed beside me. First thought he'd gone out to the ewes, then remembered all that business with Debbie in middle of the night. Went downstairs. Into kitchen. Automatically put kettle on, didn't really want a drink. He came in. Said he must have fallen asleep on the sofa. He looked pretty rough.

I was still thinking only about Debbie and that he must be as worried about her as I was. What sort of Christmas she was going to have, and birthday. What we could possibly do to help her through it. Felt a real pang, not for her, but touched that he cared about her so much.

I offered him a drink, turned away, got mugs out. He must have been in agony. Seeing all those familiar things – our things – the mugs, I'll never forget, the jokey one I bought at the Royal, the other with the kingfishers on. Seeing me put them down like I've done hundreds, thousands of times before, in our ordinary lives. Then he started to tell me.

Even then – even then, I didn't realise.

When he said he'd been having an affair, I said I knew. I did, didn't I? But I was wrong. It's not that sort of affair.

No good. Can't write any more.

5 p.m. Have slept a bit, was awake all night, tears, turning it over. Can't take it in.

Incredible how something so long-awaited can take you so totally by surprise. But I was waiting for the wrong thing. Looking in completely the wrong direction. And that made it so much worse. I felt – feel – such a fool. More stupid than if I hadn't realised anything. I thought I knew him, thought I could read him, read the signs, but I'm completely illiterate. I know nothing at all.

I couldn't breathe. I was gasping, couldn't get my breath. I thought he'd killed me.

The pain is physical. People talk about being winded, wounded. At first I couldn't even cry. Can now. Endlessly. But then, when I opened my mouth, all that came out was this awful, low, animal sound, like people make in films when they've been hit.

I don't know what happened next. He was fussing, offering me blankets, brandy. I couldn't have him near me, ran out. Was sick, or wanted to be, retching. He must have gone and found Debbie, she came. I didn't know she knew. But – oh, god, poor love – she was the one who found him out.

It was at Freddie and Lily's party. Siobhan was there with the baby, and Debbie just – knew. She tackled Elizabeth and then she tackled Brian. And so he told me.

What Debbie must have gone through. This on top of Simon.

She has run farm single-handedly all weekend. Thank God Alice with Holly till tomorrow. Brian shut in office with whisky. Pokes head out whenever I go down, says we need to talk.

Saying what?

8 p.m. Debbie made bit of supper for us both, can't be bothered. Asked me what I'm going to do.

Have no idea. Not just the past that's gone, but the future. Terror, sheer sick terror.

His other affairs were nothing compared to this. She's given him a son. How can this ever be over, when she's given him a son?

Debbie furious, says I've given him daughters, granddaughters. Not the same, and she knows it.

I had a certainty of sorts, or thought I did. It wasn't – like for some – the certainty that he'd never stray. I knew Brian wasn't faithful, but I thought he was loyal. So I accommodated his wanderings. They'd have made some women insecure, but they were my security. Because I tolerated them, I kept him coming back. But I don't see how that's going to work this time.

What am I going to do? Fight it? With what?

Brian now in kitchen, banging around. Don't think he'll dare come up here. Will have to talk tomorrow. Must. Must sort something out before Alice comes home, she mustn't know.

How could he. How could he?

Don't know how we're going to do this.

But – he hasn't gone to her.

Monday 16th December

12 p.m. Talked to Brian. He loves her.

He loves me too, he says.

What is going to happen to us?

4 p.m. Went to bed this afternoon, cried a lot. Alice home any minute. At least Brian has showered and shaved. David called this morning, Debbie sent him through to Brian, said he should see him for what he is. She is surprising me. So hard.

Car on drive. Alice home.

7 p.m. Managed awkward supper, the four of us. Debbie will only talk to Brian about the farm or in front of Alice. Alice babbling about Phil's Carols by Candlelight. Can't see how any of us can possibly carry on, especially not with Christmas. Feel sick at thought.

12 a.m. Made self talk to Brian again. He told David this morning, so David'll tell Ruth. And Elizabeth knows – and Nigel. Full shame and indignity still dawning.

More facts. They sort of help.

He's been seeing her for over a year – well, I could have worked that out, with the baby. He denies the affair was what broke up her marriage. Ruairi was, he says, an accident. An accident!

Over a year. And I only began to pick up on things in September, not even then really. I'm losing my touch. You'd have thought, with this being so – serious – there'd have been different things to pick up on. Sad, really, that even for a real love affair it's still the same glib excuses.

Except that time – November – the night he just gabbled something. Because he'd brought her and the baby home from hospital. That message I caught him playing back – the walk and whisky night – she was ringing to tell him she was in labour. All next day he was with her – how he dared – but he wasn't there for the birth. He had to leave because we were due at Grey Gables. He must have hated me that night. And the next day he brought them out and he couldn't bring himself to leave them.

He loves her and my god, he loves that baby. Oh, and me too, supposedly.

It can't be. It just can't.

He can't have both of us. Not any more. Told him so.

Her or me. Choose.

Tuesday 17th December

2 p.m. He's gone to see her, to 'talk things through'. He told me because, he says, he doesn't want to lie to me any more. If he doesn't come back, he won't have to.

6 p.m. Brian back.

wednesday 18th December

4 p.m. Exhausted after yesterday. Talking to Alice at lunch, the effort of simply keeping my head upright almost too much. She and Debbie went for a ride, went to bed again. Thought a lot, cried.

Brian won't tell me what was said yesterday. Suppose technically this is 'not lying to me' but hardly much of an improvement. He's going to see her again Friday afternoon. A deadline. His? Hers? What's he going to do? What's he going to do? Have to think. What can I do?

10.30 p.m. Have spent all evening cooking for staff drinks on Friday. Have told Brian am going to widen it to include all friends and relatives. He is horrified. It's a risk. It could backfire.

Thursday 19th December

12 p.m. Alice gone Christmas shopping all day – Brian at accountant – definite appointment, then NFU Christmas lunch (I hope but how do I know?) – Debbie overhauling tractor.

House to myself all morning. Can't settle. Wandering round. Looking at all our things. Everything that would be broken up. The sitting room, the honeysuckle work fireplace that Brian had restored when he first moved in. The pictures, the sofas, the cabinet of Beswick Pottery bulls. Helping him move in, the housewarming, him standing with his arm round me, advising Tony the secret of making it homely, I'd told him, was cushions.

The dining room, my kitchen. All the meals cooked and served at that table. Bringing the babies back here, through the back door, past the bootjack and the Barbours, Kate, Alice. Alice in her bouncing chair on the quarry tiles, laughing in that little broderie anglaise dress Mum bought her. Brian said she looked like the Pope. The yard, the cars, the Range Rover. The grain silos, the ewes in the field near the house, the earliest of the earlies already inside. The deer shed, the workshop, even the diesel pump. Is he going to let it all go? The swimming pool, covered. Brian in his old sunhat, with fishing net, complaining he's the only one who ever scoops the leaves out. Kate lolling, saying pool attendant suits him. Adam and Brian playing cricket on the lawn, Adam only ten.

Debbie, barefoot, stepping on that broken milk bottle. Brian, ashen, rushing her to have stitches, his introduction to family life. Is he going to do it all again with someone else? If so, why's he still here?

I love this photo — Alice is about a day old.

Not even a week since all this happened. Can't believe it. Like a blank behind me, and even bigger blank in front.

So frightened. He still loves me, he says, but he loves her too. And she has the baby. How can that possibly balance out? I have our past, but he can't think that's worth very much, or he'd never have let things go this far. He says he didn't mean any of it to happen — as if that makes it all right, put it in the passive, not his fault. He let it happen. He must have wanted it.

If he hadn't come back the other day, what would I have done? I did think about it, had to. And all I could think was how I was going to present it to people. Terrible, makes me feel so shallow. How could I be more concerned with the form than the feeling? But I was.

That's what gave me the party idea. Not just that if I could convince everyone that everything was all right, I could convince myself, and perhaps Brian too. Not just about showing him everything we'd built together and what was threatened if he pulled it down, collapsed it, a house of cards. Not just my public face. But realising that in all the humiliation, and so many people knowing – oh yes, not just Ruth and David, and Elizabeth and Nigel, but Shula and Alistair, apparently (I went and asked Elizabeth) and Janet and Tim (well, of course, I should have realised) – not Phil and Jill, though, thank god – realising I had to have my dignity, had to do things my own way, properly. So no one, least of all me, could reproach me for anything.

Going for walk. Millennium Wood perfect, never anyone there. Crying in open air feels different, freer.

Friday 20th December

2 p.m. Brian gone to Felpersham.

Been to shop for more paracetamol. Have taken more this past week than in entire rest of life. Debbie thinks I need Valium, or sleeping pills. Not so long ago I was wondering the same for her. Tried to talk to her about how she's feeling. She says she's 'dealing with it'.

Shop surreal – Christmas decorations, fake snow in window, children's selection boxes piled up everywhere. Jean Harvey nagging Betty about shelled walnuts. Can't comprehend that for rest of village, life is going on as normal. Seems obscene, somehow.

Walked to shop, don't trust self to drive. Concentration zero. Have to conserve it for conversations with Alice. Will have to pep self up by tonight.

One good thing out of all this, weight has dropped off. Not wearing the trouser outfit I bought last month, but red Max Mara haven't been able to get into for two years.

Have done as much forward preparation as I can – catering, that is. (Freezer is bulging, just canapés to prepare.) Am doing two levels of food, nice stuff for us, also going to lay paté, cheese, bread etc. buffet type thing in dining room for likes of Jeff, Andy, Greg. Drinks came this morning, Brian helped me lay them out, not saying much. Debbie came in, said he ought to try and enjoy it, it might be the last party he ever came to at Home Farm. Brian literally cringed.

Have to talk to Debbie though. Don't think she can understand that isn't what I want. I know what I do want. Have known all along, really.

Sounds crazy. I hate him for what he's done, but I love him.

5 p.m. Alice and Holly – invited for tonight – helped do flowers, make filo parcels, etc. this afternoon, kept my mind off things – like, will Brian actually be here? Mum and Jack have promised to be early, help with last-minute stuff. Debbie clearly dreading the party, her first public appearance since Simon, but says she can do it if I can.

Told her that I definitely want to make our marriage work. She looked incredulous. All depends on Brian, anyway.

Brian not back yet.

7 p.m. Where is he? Guests due 7.30. This party could be bigger test of my dignity than I was anticipating.

Have had stiff gin. Alice caught me swigging, thought I was in for one of her lectures on evils of alcohol, but she said she understood, it was equivalent of horse having a 'pipe-opener' at a point-to-point. She's being very sweet. Don't think she's detected anything between Brian and I. Think she assumes he and Debbie have had a row about the farm. Debbie uneasy about this, thinks it's another deceit, but has to be better than the truth surely?

Where is he? Feel like today will never end.

12 a.m. It's over.

Saturday 21st December

8 a.m. Actually slept, must have been sheer exhaustion/relief.

Brian really cranked up the tension, didn't arrive back till gone eight, loads of people here already, then let out he'd been in Felpersham in front of Alice. Had to save his skin with excuse about Christmas shopping. He had look of a stunned calf, what does that woman do to him?

Made sure I talked to everyone – Jill, Phil, Shula, Alistair, Caroline, Oliver, Snells, Beesboroughs. Headache banging away. Everyone enjoyed food, especially David who consumed almost entire plate of filo parcels by himself. Brian lurked by drinks table most of the night, talking to/being talked at by Jack. Debbie closeted with Elizabeth in morning room quite a while. Poor angel.

One really bad moment, Shula talking about Caroline and Oliver's romantic trip to Rome. Made me think of our trip to Hungary with them, the meal we had in that restaurant the first night and me ticking Brian off for talking about farming – what about the food, the wine, the romance? 'All right, darling,' he said, 'you'll get your romance.' And I did, he was lovely to me the whole time. When I know now I was second best.

Alice and I tidying up after party, Debbie gone back to cottage when Brian came to help – something of a first. Packed Alice off to bed. Brian said something about helping me clear up in the morning. Long pause. Then we talked.

He's staying. Or says he is.

Going for bath.

11 a.m. No sign of Brian, note saying he's gone out to see to the ewes, though I know Debbie's already seen to them this morning.

It's weird, isn't it, that when you think you've got to the end of something, it's really only another beginning? Like Brian's telling me about the affair – though it felt like the end of everything – was really only the end of one stage and the start of the next. And now he/I/we've come to a decision about the future, the next stage is making it happen.

Because if he's staying, he has to give her up. It was extraordinary, when I said it last night he looked as though I'd run him through with a knife. I can't believe he hadn't seen that the one necessarily follows from the other. It seems perfectly logical to me. He just seemed – winded. Long, long pause, then he said in tiny voice that he'd try. Try! That's big of him.

But now – I assume – he's thinking about it. How – and if – he can.

Sunday 22nd December

9 a.m. Writing it like that, a few words on a page, makes it seem so simple. Our conversation about it was anything but. God knows what it'll be like when he tries to talk to her. She's bound to put up some kind of a fight. Is he strong enough?

The trouble is, she has so much going for her. I may seem to have all the cards: the marriage, the commitment, the history. But what am I really playing with? Or hoping to play on? Kindness, conscience, nostalgia – not exactly feelings which Brian has in spades. The moral high ground then – his sense of duty? Well, yes, in theory that should work: of course Brian's a traditionalist – a conservative – why else would having a son be so important to him? But how appealing is duty compared with adventure – a new life – a younger woman – his longed-for son? She's everything freshly minted, a new start, just for him. What am I? More of the same.

Can't believe I'm going through all this again. It's not as if it's the first time. Which of course has made it a thousand times worse. I'm not just

75

dealing with this, it's made me excavate the whole Caroline thing again. How so painfully slowly, after that, before anything could grow back, the distance between us had to grow less. But it did. Bit by painful bit, normality returned – sheer habit and politeness at first. Then a gradual unbending on my part to let him get close again. The first time I allowed myself to laugh at some joke he made – the first time he dared make a joke – the first time I let him go off the farm without checking when he'd be back. Making myself stop rifling through his wallet. Even the glove box of the car. Ridiculous, because it was over by then anyway, supposedly. But that's it. Supposedly. Like he's supposedly going to stop seeing her.

Don't know whether all this crying is sorrow, or anger coming out as sorrow. Feel so, so cheated.

In obvious sense of betrayal, of course – the length of time it had been going on, the deceit, it's detail, it's deliberateness. Almost a callous enjoyment of it, on his part – the satisfaction he must have felt at having got away with it for so long, and so often! Those elaborate excuses – why? There was no need, I was so dim. That first time he stayed out all night, in July? Supposedly had too much to drink? And I believed him? She'd been burgled, apparently, he 'couldn't leave her on her own'. What! He's never minded leaving me on my own! Then the bloody Countryside March – I feel such a fool. He'd been with her the whole weekend, of course – then on the Sunday she had some fainting fit, hence the Filofax story. I knew it, I knew. Oh, and the shooting in Scotland which I find out was really a nice little break in Biarritz? But the tweeds he appeared home in? He changed in the Felpersham Travelodge. And the grouse he brought back? Bought them. Oh, and there's more, so many more. I made him tell me. And I've been back through my entire diary, piecing together precisely how he took me apart.

And it's stupid and childish, I know, but on top of everything, I feel so resentful. Here am I having to cope with all this rubbish – I didn't ask for any of it – and I didn't even have any of the fun! It's so unfair!

Was our relationship that bad?

12 p.m. Have been living in such a strange world, moving in slow motion as if under water, and all muffled. When I went to village on Friday, cars seemed frightening, aggressively fast, tractors like tanks, mud spraying up violently from puddles. Feel like someone who's been in sanatorium for six months.

Christmas three days away and have done nothing towards food, have hardly wrapped a present. Mum just rang to ask if she and Jack could bring anything, had to drag mind round to what she might be talking about. Finally dawned on me they're coming for Christmas lunch. Will have to find energy to write list, get Underwoods or supermarket to deliver. Also have usual Boxing Day shoot (for Matt Crawford of all people) but have told Brian cannot possibly do sit-down lunch, they will have to have picnic at one of the drives.

Part of me can't believe I'm doing all this, carrying on with Christmas, feeding his shooting party. Debbie says I should mount House of Atreus-style expose of him in front of the guns – or possibly she means with a gun – she seems so murderous towards Brian at the moment, wouldn't put anything past her. If not that, she favours poisoned casserole or perhaps shirt of Nessus, can see her crushing up foxgloves and sewing them in seams of his tweed jacket. Have told her no. How I – we, supposedly – want to stay married. She paid me compliment of saying I'm being incredibly strong, but can't help thinking she thinks I'm actually incredibly feeble. Wonder myself. I've every reason to throw him out, make a public example of him. Except that the humiliation would kill me. And – so wish I didn't – I do still love him.

2 p.m. Asked Brian about lunch, said he didn't want anything. Have hardly seen him all weekend. He seems as out of it as I am. Am getting very scared. Wish I knew what he was thinking. Has retreated to office again, though not with whisky, thankfully. Terrified. What if he's changed his mind, is going to her?

Carols by Candlelight tonight. Dreading it, but have to go for Alice. Realise had been pacing self for party, now am wrung out again. And this is the Christmas (and birthday) I was supposed to be making nice for Debbie. Now effort got be made for Alice too, well, everyone, really. Assuming there is still a Christmas to have as a family.

5 p.m. Didn't think this weekend could possibly be worse than last, somehow it's managed to be.

Have been wrapping presents all afternoon. Seems like I bought them in another life. Will have no chance now to get into Borchester for all the 'extras' on Alice's list, she'll have to go without. Make it up to her with more cash or something.

Spent ages looking at presents I'd bought Brian. Those cufflinks I took so long choosing. Folding and refolding the sweater, cashmere, that beautiful buttery yellow. Thought of all the clothes I'd washed and ironed, folded for him in the past year. The buttons sewn on, the socks paired. Him asking me specially before the Countryside March weekend to press his linen trousers, also his favourite navy shirt. And I did it. And it was for her.

Got to get ready for carols.

12 a.m. Too hyper to sleep.

Can't believe Brian. Furious. He just seems so dense in all this. Adds a whole new level to my rage – why am I having to mastermind it all?? None of it will be any good if he's just acting on my orders. He has to want to do what he says he's going to do, but as for how to achieve it, he seems to have the mental agility of a man in a coma. He's usually so incisive, decisive. I know, of course I know, this is hardly the same as forward-selling grain or when to vaccinate the ewes, but even so...

I know why he's like it, of course I do. It's because he really cares about her – and about Ruairi.

His timing is incredible, though.

Gone five, just as Alice was about to go down to St Stephen's for the final run-through, and about half an hour before we should have been going ourselves, he came and found me. Said he wanted to talk. I was a bit sharp with him – sheer dread of what he was going to say – but it was

OK to begin with. He said he got the feeling I hadn't quite given up on him and me, but he knew there was one condition attached – and he said I was right. If we were going to stay together and rebuild things, he'd have to give her up, end it. I didn't even have a fraction of a second to savour it, though. Because then he said he couldn't give up Ruairi.

It was incredible. Mars and Venus in my own sitting room. He really seemed to think that, having said he wouldn't see her again, I was going to let him see her, but with the baby as the excuse! As if that makes any difference! The baby's been there for the past month, for goodness' sake, that didn't stop it being an affair! Next he'll be suggesting we all set up house together! He's spent the past 48 hours thinking about this. This is what he's come up with – and he expects me blithely to accept it?

No, no, NO.

1. The baby's a package deal with her. What did he think she was going to do, leave him outside in his buggy for Brian to collect every Saturday morning? What planet is he on, as Alice would say. And what, pray, would Brian do on his own in Felpersham with a baby? As if he'd have a clue. What if it was raining?

2. So that's not going to work. How can it possibly be over, then, I put to him, if he's still seeing her on a regular basis, playing happy families or even just for some kind of 'handover'? His answer? That I should trust him!

3. He then tried to say that I of all people should 'understand' that he wants to see Ruairi. Excuse me, but I hardly think it's the time for him to start playing the 'let's patronise single parents' card!

He tried to take it back, said he knew how painful my experience had been for me etc., but I gave him the benefit of my 'pain' – told him straight out he'd be much better off making a clean break. And he would, for everyone, I don't just mean that for me. You've only got to look at Debbie and Adam to see that.

He said he couldn't.

And then we got stuck again. He certainly wasn't offering any solutions. So it was down to me.

The only way I can see this working – the ONLY way – and then it's a huge maybe – is if she moves completely away from here. I just know that with her twenty minutes down the road, and knowing how much he wants contact with the baby, I could never, ever relax. Every time he went off the farm, every time he was half an hour late back – I'd be beside myself, thinking 'Is this it? Has he gone for good?' I don't care how he does it, but he's got to make her see that she's going to have to leave. And if she will, then – I don't know – maybe, over time, he could see Ruairi, what, every month or so? – and maybe I could go with him, sit in the car while Brian collected him and she'd have to let us have him for the day, or a few hours, or whatever we decide. But I do know that's the only way I could possibly cope with it.

Told him so. Got the landed fish expression again. How, he asked, is he to make her move away? Not my problem! I felt like saying. Except it is.

So then he asked me what would happen if he couldn't persuade her. Or if she won't go. And it came out of my mouth, pat, just like that. It wasn't exactly rehearsed. But I've been thinking about it, of course, non-stop, in the abstract. What it would mean, for me, for us. Divorce.

But when I had to spell it out – that Alice would stay with me, that the farm would have to be sold and split, that Debbie would be out of a job – it was the quickest reaction I've had out of him since this blew up. 'I don't want that,' he said at once. 'I don't want any of it.' Well, fine. He's got to think again, then, about this cock-eyed scheme for keeping in touch with Ruairi. He's got to think about all his children, what's best for all of them.

So, somewhat bloodied, we trooped off to Carols by Candlelight. And joined the happy throng.

Monday 23rd December

2 p.m. Brian went to see her this morning. Longest morning I've ever known. Supermarket delivery van here 8 a.m., groaning. Peeled mountain of chestnuts – far too many – for stuffing. Made carrot and parsnip mash, cranberry sauce, bread sauce. Even did sprouts, far too early for Wednesday, even though now in iced water, but don't care, just want to be occupied.

Always going through my head: 'I'm not going to get away with this. She's not going to give him up, she's not the type. Siobhan Hathaway, flame-haired temptress, retreating to lick her wounds, lying down and dying? Especially when she's got the baby to bargain with?' And yet I've gone and staked everything on it. Told him what the alternative is – that was clever. What if he calls my bluff? Could I really go through with it?

Hands shaking, stomach churning. Lord knows who'll eat all this food. Not me.

But by 12 – far earlier than I expected – he was home. But – funny – so little's changed since it was all their big secret. I only know what he's prepared to tell me, which isn't much.

All I know is, he's told her it's over. She seems to have accepted it – or at least he seems to think she has, no going back. But about arrangements to see Ruairi, or moving away – I don't know if anything was resolved. He 'mentioned it', he said. But as to what she said in reply, he wouldn't tell me. Said he had to be on his own. Hid in the office again. Another bottle of Bourbon.

Am I any further forward?

Tuesday 24th December

Debbie's birthday today.

There is a God. As her present, Alice has come up with panto tickets for herself and Debbie tonight, so no need to put on false show of bonhomie/elaborate birthday meal. Oh, thank you, thank you. Thank God also this year's panto is 'Little Red Riding Hood', not 'Cinderella' or 'Sleeping Beauty' or any one involving handsome prince.

Brian shut in office all yesterday afternoon. Today, as birthday present to Debbie, not that she was impressed, he's insisting on doing all the stock. Simply said to me he wanted to keep busy. Has his mobile with him, of course. If she's still speaking to him.

Have no idea, really, how things were left between them, if she's still going to make a play for him, make it impossible for him to extricate self. She has such a strong weapon with the baby, she must know she has. Can't believe she won't use it.

All he's promised is that he'll be here for Christmas – and his precious shoot, presumably. Can't miss that!

Feel in total, total despair. Fog. No idea how we're going to get through tomorrow, any of us. Debbie seems very low. She doesn't agree with my giving Brian another chance. Says she gave Simon another chance, and look what happened, all men are bastards, etc.

Sometimes I hurt for her more than for me. Not just Simon and Brian betraying her, but me too, encouraging her to try again with Simon. Telling her, even, and meaning it at the time – fool! – that a little infidelity can strengthen a marriage. Will never forgive myself.

Wish now had gone to doctor for Valium.

Wednesday 25th December
Christmas Day

Worst Christmas of my life. Was bad enough when Brian told me but Christmas has been worse.

Appalling falseness about whole day, am sure Mum suspects something. Presents, lunch, agony of play-acting. Debbie so brittle, thought she'd break. Neither of us could bring ourselves to open Brian's presents.

He gave me an eternity ring.

Thursday 26th December
Boxing Day

Don't know what came over me today. It began like they all do now, sort of dead feeling inside, indifferently packing cold turkey, sausages, mayonnaise, pickles, into cool bags, heating soup, making vats of coffee. Guns arrived about nine thirty, coffee, mince pies, cherry brandy at the house and they drew pegs. Matt C. immediately grumbling about his, ridiculous as he knows they all move along during the day, so everyone gets to shoot from the centre as well as the end pegs. Brian scowling.

Took lunch out in Range Rover just after one, Debbie and Alice helping. Guns hadn't had a good morning, suspect most of them liverish after yesterday, probably DTs as well, so their aim not too hot. That's what Brian implied anyway. Started unpacking lunch, Matt immediately smarmed up, usual line of what a perfect wife I was, Yvette fretful over sinful consumption of calories and only waiting for shops to open again, Harvey Nicks' sale in particular.

Couldn't not be polite, so chatting away when I saw Brian give me a funny look, as if I had no right to be talking to Matt at all. Suddenly felt this boiling fury, like lava, so when Matt said some of the others wanted to meet me, abandoned the lunch and tripped off with him to chat to these other boorish types. Brian open-mouthed.

It wasn't planned, it was a spur-of-the-moment thing. God knows, there's hardly much satisfaction in being appreciated by Matt Crawford or the people he associates with, but I don't know, maybe I was trying to get back at Brian in the only pathetic way I could.

Anyway, Brian didn't let it go. Took me on one side and accused me of flirting, Debbie overheard, accused Brian of being a hypocrite, Alice came in on spat between them, Debbie had to tell Alice she and Brian had been rowing about Simon – we almost got the House of Atreus after all. My family is imploding. There'll be nothing left for her to split up soon.

Friday 27th December

11 a.m. Brian (still in 'not lying to me' mode) has gone to see Siobhan. (Done it – written her name. Maybe 'flirting' with Matt Crawford did me some good after all.) But it's only 'to see the baby'.

Have horrible feeling that somehow I've lost the advantage. A few days ago, when we talked about him giving her up and her moving, I thought I had it, but it seems to have slipped away. I thought he wasn't supposed to be seeing her again? Or only seeing the baby with me there? So how have we arrived at today?

Have I given up? At this moment, am almost too exhausted to care.

Maybe I've lost more than my advantage. What if he doesn't come home?

Monday 30th December

9 p.m. She's gone.

Couldn't write anything before, didn't dare, would have been tempting fate.

When Brian came home on Friday – late, late, God, I was frightened – he was ashen. I was terrified, assumed he'd come home to tell me the worst and pack a bag. Couldn't believe it when he sank down at the table with this tragic look, said she was going to Ireland for New Year – as always intended apparently – but not coming back, going to stay there with her family. I didn't know what to think. I couldn't believe it, couldn't believe my luck. New start, new life, yes. But without him.

I simply couldn't believe it, though Brian seemed convinced she meant it. Spent all weekend – all weekend – didn't sleep, eat, anything – trying to second-guess. Was she bluffing? Could he really stand back and let her – them – go? Nerves in shreds.

And today. He went out this morning, checked on the deer, the grain lorry came – and when I next looked, the car had gone. Suddenly a crater where my stomach should have been. And the middle of my chest tight, tight. Heartache, literally.

Flew upstairs to look in his wardrobe – what had he taken? Couldn't see much, if anything, missing – but that didn't mean anything. Not when I'd convinced myself he'd decided he couldn't let her go.

Didn't know what time her flight was, hadn't asked. Couldn't know the details, would have read too much into them. 14.10 – sounds lucky for me, he'll stay. But 15.05 – don't like the sound of that, he'll be going with her. Crazy. Crazy or what? But I am a bit mad at the moment.

Couldn't sit still. Paced the kitchen, then went and paced about on Lakey Hill. When I came back, his car in the yard. Had convinced myself he'd gone for good, thought I was hallucinating. Looked for him in with the ewes, called round the buildings, but no sign. Then Jeff said he'd seen him heading off towards the riding course with stakes and netting for the fencing that needed doing.

The first I saw of him was about an hour ago. He came in to collect his stuff for the lambing caravan – Debbie, sadistically, has made a rota for them and he's doing mostly nights. He asked where the muscle rub was. I said I gathered he'd been doing some fencing. He looked caught out. Said it was to 'take his mind off things'. I asked if she'd definitely gone, he said yes. I didn't ask where they said their goodbyes.

He looks awful, aged ten years. Debbie can't understand me, how I can feel sorry for him, still care. But I do. I'm livid with him as well, of course – I mean, that tragic face on Friday – what does he expect, sympathy? But just because this is all his own doing doesn't mean I can't feel for him, that he's suffering. I can't get out of the habit of caring, I've been doing it for too long. If I didn't care about him, none of us would be going through this, I could simply have let him go. The caring is what's made it all so much worse.

Twenty six years, gone in a sentence when he told me, or that's what I thought. But if love can survive even when a marriage is over – and it does – then it must still be there when a marriage is in trouble. It's just impossible to see it, or show it. I can't reach out to him at the moment or offer any comfort – he wouldn't take it from me anyway. But it doesn't mean I don't sometimes want to.

We do love each other, Brian and I. I know we do.

Tuesday 31st December

It's a good job I wrote all that about loving Brian yesterday, don't feel like I do today. This is what's so exhausting, like April weather, one day hopeful sun, back to icy winds the next.

He's done nothing but infuriate me today, moping around looking hangdog, moaning about having to go to the Snells' Hogmanay party tonight. I could shake him. I'm not exactly relishing the prospect myself, but, like the staff party, it's part of the 'normal life' we've agreed we're supposed to be trying to live, and anyway, Alice, at least, is looking forward to it. Keep telling him he's got to pull himself together, for her sake if nothing else.

Wednesday 1st January 2003

Most of my worst fears about last night realised, though not all of them. Lynda had gone completely over the top with her 'Braveheart' theme, making the year that Shane festooned Nelson's in Hunting Stewart look tasteful by comparison. Wisely avoided her Het Pint (most of which ended up regurgitated in her water feature) but couldn't avoid Ed Grundy's friend Jazzer's supposedly 'traditional' New Year poem, which sounded more like the sort of thing you'd hear on the streets at closing time in the Gorbals. Watched Brian like a hawk all night but no evidence of mobile phone calls made or received, and he was certainly with me at midnight. Gave me a quick peck and we even managed to say Happy New Year to one another.

Though of course he didn't need to call her, he must have spent all night thinking about last year, how different things were. Like I did. I know now why he danced with her at Lower Loxley. How clever he must have

89

thought he was! The thrill of dancing perfectly legitimately with your mistress, with your wife looking on. Felt murderous. Luckily for him he had to check on the lambing when we got in or I think I'd have physically attacked him.

Have also realised all these hours in the lambing shed are perfect cover for phone calls. After all, with a small baby, it's not exactly as if she's got a defined day/night routine. Feel desperate again. Have no idea if he's still in contact with her.

This isn't going to stop, is it?

Friday 3rd January

2 p.m. Bumped into Phil this morning. It was strange talking to someone else from outside the four of us. I could feel my mouth moving, but I wasn't sure if I was making any sense. We've been living such a bizarre, enclosed life the past fortnight – is that all it is? – all in our own little bubble. I've seen Mum and Jack, of course, and talked to people the other night at the Snells, but Phil's such a darling, so solid, so reassuring. You can't imagine him and Jill being rocked by something like this, ever.

We just chatted – about nothing, really, how Lynda seemed to have confused Hogmanay with Burns' Night and about her catty 'Echo' review of Larry Lovell's panto which ignored the production and majored instead on the new loos. And for a second, I came back from the dead and remembered what 'normal life' was actually like – and then it all came washing over me again, the shame of it, and I just wanted to scurry home and hide, even thought it's so horrible here, Brian not speaking, hardly, and Debbie not speaking to him, ever, and me gabbling all the time, covering up in front of Alice and being desperate, so desperate, and thinking it'll never, ever, get better.

I'm the last person who should be thinking like this – I'm the one who wanted us to stay together. And we should be living proof, Brian and I, that one (let's be honest, both) parties in a marriage can have an affair and it can still survive. We've survived before. But that was completely different. I was younger then, there were still things we could do about it, things we could do together. We went on to have Alice, for a start, hardly an option that's available to me now. What have we got to look forward to this time? Tottering into the sunset on our Zimmer frames, smacking our lips at a nice cod mornay for supper (bland yet tasty, no nasty bones) and trying to time our respective cataract operations so one can look after the other?

Think I might give up this diary. Sometimes I wonder if it's making me worse.

6 p.m. Some New Year resolution that was. Trouble is, if I don't put it down here, I don't know where all this emotion would go.

Debbie's just announced she's thinking of going to the Oxford Farming Conference next week, away Sunday to Thursday, missing my birthday. Had to tell her I don't mind, but was already dreading it. Alice is bound to go overboard and make a fuss and Brian's already asked me what I want to do – oh, I know, I felt like saying, let's invite that nice Siobhan Hathaway round to dinner, shall we? Also felt like pointing out we might not actually make it to January 7th. In the end, Mum suggested we wind it in with their anniversary and have dinner at Grey Gables, thank God. At least it means Brian and I won't have to be that agonising couple – there's one in every restaurant – who have nothing to say to each other and spend needless hours studying the menu and the rest of the meal occasionally commenting on the wallpaper.

Debbie tried to persuade me that I needed a break too, bless her. As if I'd dare. Look what happened last year.

I was so thrilled, so naively pleased when Brian booked me into that health farm, thinking he must have remembered it was the one Lilian had raved about. I can see him now, waving me off – and all the time he was just thinking about how soon he could get into bed with her. And yet he put on that show of being all over me, taking me out to Grey Gables when I got back, smarming round... guilty conscience, I suppose. That's when we arranged for me to go to Hungary. And then look how he tried to put me off, telling me there were no shops, it'd be freezing cold. He'd gone off the idea of my boring company by then. We all know who he'd rather have taken with him for the gypsy violins and spiced wine beneath the castle walls.

I hate him, I hate him for doing this, not just to me, but to all of us. Told Debbie she must go to Oxford, anyway.

Sunday 5th January

9.30 p.m. Couldn't not go to Janet Fisher's leaving do. Knew it'd be a strain and it was, knowing Janet knows, also Elizabeth and Shula in a huddle, talking about me, I expect, as well they might be. Realise E. was very friendly with Siobhan, though would have hoped loyalty to Debbie, if not to me, would have made her cut Siobhan off once she knew what was going on. Know Debbie feels that way. She has dropped Elizabeth like a stone, won't speak to her. For me, actually feel worse about Shula. This isn't the first time she's known about one of Brian's affairs. Would love to know how she squares it all with her Christian conscience.

Brian in lambing caravan. Going for bath.

10.30 p.m. But would I tell Shula if Alistair was having an affair? Yes, I think I would. Feel thoroughly let down. Bad enough Tim knowing all along when I didn't (and then Janet), but half family complicit in it as well.

Also selfishly resentful that Tim – the other 'innocent party' – is able to walk away, as if from wreckage of a car crash – while I'm still trapped in it. And happily make new life with Janet.

Sick of feeling sorry for self.

Monday 6th January
Not a good day. Still very low. Dreading tomorrow.

Tuesday 7th January
My birthday. Was right to dread it. Horrendous. Surely can't go any lower?

Wednesday 8th January
Yes, can actually.

Thursday 9th January

'King Lear', isn't it? 'The worst is not; so long as we can say, "This is the worst".'

Really thought I'd gone as low as I could at various points over the last few weeks – when he told me, that first weekend – then the next weekend, waiting for him to decide if he could give her up – Christmas Day – then yet another horrendous weekend, waiting for her to go – New Year's Eve – the whole timing of this thing couldn't have been worse. But on my birthday – well, I hit whole new series of lows. (Can you hit a low? Implies height, somehow. All right, sank to. Brain just not working. First vocabulary gone, grammar and syntax next, probably. Am losing my mind, and no wonder.)

Perhaps the mistake was going to Janet's leaving party. Too many people, things, to feel resentful about. Left me with bilious bitterness, towards life, Brian, everything.

Terrible state all Monday. Hated him with a ferocity I didn't think I had the capacity for. How could he do this to me? To us? Alice's last day of school holidays, had to stand over her while she did her homework, all left to last minute of course, then slog into Borchester for protractor, new copy of Anita Desai as she's lost the school one. W.H. Smith like first circle of hell, sale on, endless queues, people stupidly trying to swop books and CDs they'd had for Christmas, wanting to scream, 'You're lucky to have had a normal Christmas, don't you realise? I wish all I had to think about was what Aunty So-and-So gave me!' Nearly fainting by time reached till, so hot in there. Staggered back to car, put head down on steering wheel and wept.

Birthday came. Alice's first day back at school. Mum round first thing to give me present – pen, beautiful, using it now. Alice, the sweetheart, had made me a cake, sneaked round to The Lodge Sunday evening, made it there. Chocolate inevitably. Nearly threw up. Brian in from lambing to take Alice to school but she wheedled lift out of mum. Left me with Brian sooner than I wanted. Didn't actually want to be on my own with him at all.

Not proud of what happened next, but had been a long time coming.

He gave me his present. Beautifully wrapped – by the girl in Underwoods, of course. Perfume. And then the card. 'I have always loved you'. And I just – erupted. All that fury, all the pent-up humiliation, rage, scorn and the utter, utter hurt and betrayal of it all. Threw the perfume on the floor – terrible stink. Instant headache, like fist in left eyeball. And then shouting and screaming at him about Siobhan being a whore, and how he treated me like a doormat, how a man like him who couldn't keep his hands off other women should never have married, how he was greedy and selfish, didn't think about anyone else as long as he got what he wanted, how I should have known I could never be enough. Out and out of my mouth, all this bile, like something out of *The Exorcist*. On and on, couldn't seem to stop. Brian kept saying he meant it. He had always loved me. More he said it, worse it got. So it ended up with me crying (again) and him insisting it was true, he'd always loved me, that had never changed. Hah! What if it's changed for me, though?

Walked out. Didn't know where I was going, don't know what I'd have done if I'd met anyone, thank god I didn't. Must have looked like madwoman. Only tiny scrap of old tissue in pocket, had to blow nose on scarf. Dreadful. Found self on Lakey Hill. Blowing a gale, trying to rain. Saw Phil and Heather, Ruth's mum, with Jet in distance, trying to attract my attention. Walked on. And on. Out for hours. Crying about everything. Me and Brian, Brian and her, Brian and Debbie, Debbie and Simon. Everything just hopeless. Rebuild marriage? How? Why? For what? Felt had nothing to build on. Walked till legs felt wobbly. Sat down, grass wet, frozen. Head on knees. Felt like giving up. Fifty-eight and I'm supposed to be starting again. Feeling I'm too old for this. Must have sat there for hours.

Suddenly remembered Alice, school, got to collect her. Gone one already. Got up, nearly fell down, light-headed. No food all day. Had to keep swallowing, yawning, to stop self keeling over. Somehow got home – half an hour's walk, usually – took over an hour. Got in, made tea, toast, thawed out a bit. Still felt weird but had to get to school. Drove very slowly. Luckily Alice full of school, marks for geography project, etc. Wanted birthday cake when she got in, also Brian to come in for lighting of candles, thank god he had sense to maintain couldn't leave lambing shed.

Before left for Grey Gables, Debbie rang. Having good time at Oxford, going to stay away a few more days. Told her good for her but was desolate.

Felt like absolute death. Tried best with terrible puffy eyes but no good. Mum looked horrified as soon as she saw me. Able to goad Brian a bit with news of Debbie not coming back yet, then Mum asked what he'd given me for birthday. I said perfume, then we both gave different answers as to why I wasn't wearing it. Knew then I wouldn't be able to keep it from Mum much longer.

She was round here the minute I got back from school run yesterday. No hiding any of it – poor thing looked ghastly herself, said she hadn't slept a wink for worrying. She knew it was about Brian.

Told her. Poor Mum, she doesn't need this, at her age. Told her all about Debbie finding out, Siobhan, the baby – could see she could hardly take it in. Know that feeling. She could see at once how not just awful for me, but Debbie too. And she says Alice is unsettled, she'd said something when Mum drove her to school.

Mum wonderful. So strong. Really buoyed me up. Says I'm to ring her night or day, whenever I need her. Said if I really do want to mend things with Brian, she'll support me – though not sure she thinks I'm doing the right thing (in fact, sure she doesn't). But says I'm a survivor, like her, like dear old Granny P. and that we'll get through it. Not sure yet how, but somehow.

Feel such relief at having told her. Can't talk to Debbie about any of it anymore, she so can't understand why Brian should have another chance, says he's had all the chances he deserves, and more. But there's so much she can't see – how could she, at her age? For me, it's not about ending a two-year marriage – not that I'm making light of what she's going through, it's desperate. But it's not just Brian and me I've got to think about – there's Alice, the farm, the whole set-up. Debbie argues that plenty of other women in my position chuck their husbands out, but in the end, they're not me. She keeps saying I should do what's right for me, but as I keep trying to tell her, as far as I'm concerned this is right for me. I may not have known Brian as well as I thought I did, and I've got to live with that, but I do know myself.

Anyway, even if we were in agreement, I can't burden Debbie with all my traumas, she's got enough of her own. But, Mum, bless her, understood straight away how I feel. She knows a bit about holding your head up, all those years at the pub with dad. Has promised not to tell a soul, not even Jack. Gave me a big hug, we had a little cry. Then she went and tore into Brian!

Don't know what was said but imagine horsewhipping came into it somewhere – or perhaps she thinks that'd be too good for him. Anyway, he hardly showed his face in the house all day yesterday or today, but when he came in for socks, etc. tonight – he really is stuck with all the night shifts with Debbie still away – he was pretty subdued. Said he wished I'd mentioned before Grey Gables about her staying on in Oxford – well, why should I? He's had enough secrets, and rather more fundamental ones, if you ask me. And then – then he had the nerve to ask why I'd told mum! How about because it's about time I decided who knows what, for a change? And because it's a help to have someone on my side? Anyway, didn't go into all that. And he wouldn't be drawn. Just took his stuff, said he'd see me in the morning. And then, as he was leaving, in this little voice: 'I've lost something, too, you know'.

Friday 10th January

6 p.m. Have spent all today thinking things through. The way I behaved on my birthday really shocked me. Didn't recognise myself. What Brian said the other night rocked me, too. Talking it through with Mum has helped – and, in a sense, it's been helpful having Debbie away. Her reaction's been so extreme and I'm so aware of it, it almost gets in the way.

Whatever, have come to the conclusion that we can't go on like this. If I'm serious about rebuilding things with Brian, I've got to get my act together and at least allow for some kind of truce. I've got to put in something towards this 'normal life' we've agreed we're supposed to be leading. I can't go on holding myself away from him like I've been doing, being a thorough misery and either being cold towards him or scratching at him the rest of the time. I'm not saying I'm forgiving him, god, no. I'm not saying I'm anywhere near ready – I don't know at this stage when I ever will be. But we've got to try and get back to some kind of neutrality, because I can see that if things go on as horribly as they are, there's a real danger I'll drive him away – lose what I'm supposed to be trying to save. What he said the other night is haunting me. If I carry on like I have been, especially this week, I'm going to make him miss what he's lost even more.

Easy to say, I know, not so easy to do, but, fine, decision made: I at least have to try. But having made this great leap, I was completely stuck on how this momentous change was going to come about. Then – who'd have thought it – it was the website to the rescue.

Switched on the computer for first time since before Christmas and had 27 e-mails – not including the junk and a lovely long one from Kate – all of them gripes about the 'Ambridge Archive'. Couldn't believe it, serves me right for putting my e-mail address on there in the first place, I suppose. All sorts of grumbles, why hadn't the site been updated, how they'd hoped for a proper Christmas section, why no photos of snowdrops on Lakey Hill – endless stream of whingeing. Thoroughly fed up about it till I realised it could be the answer.

I can't bring myself to get close to Brian, I'm still far too churned up for that. (Of course I am – it's four weeks to the day since he told me.) I know the best thing would be for us to talk about it all, and I'd love to, but Brian's not having any of it – he's told me what happened, painted in the details I asked for – and some I didn't, thanks very much – told me he still loves me. Well, 'that's enough feelings (Ed.)', as far as he's concerned. It's infuriating – there's so much more I'd love to say – but this is the man, remember, who called our family therapy sessions with Kate a bigger waste of time than EU Agriculture Policy and whose answer when I confronted him about Caroline was to say: 'But it's over!'

No point dwelling on it, it's too frustrating. I've decided the best way forward is to throw myself into something else so I'm not channelling all this negative emotion at him all the time. Instead – this is the theory anyway – I put all my energies into the website – and anything else that's going on in the village – i.e. I really do 'carry on as normal'. And what I'm hoping is that when I look up again in however many months' time, I – we – still have a marriage – one I haven't poisoned with my bitterness – and we're at a place where we can start to move on together. Right now, it's enough that we're moving on at all – if not together exactly, then at least not apart. That's the plan, anyhow, and it's the best I can come up with. I'm going to give it a go.

RECONSTRUCTION

Saturday 11th January

Debbie home last night, in time to help with beaters' shoot today. Lovely to see her, though she doesn't look any better than when she went.

Wish I knew what is going through her head. She just won't talk to me. She helped with last minute food preps, took lunch out in Range Rover. Mike Tucker crowing about having Brian beating for them, Greg looking sour as usual. George commented Brian was looking under the weather, managed to cover by saying he hadn't been getting much sleep what with lambing and Debbie away. Felt virtuous and was rewarded by Brian commenting as he helped me pack up that I seemed brighter than of late. Told him that had resolved to try to look forward, not back, hoped he was doing the same. He gave a thin smile.

Sunday 12th January

On tack of throwing myself into things, went to church in Penny Hassett, taken by retired priest now we are without vicar, offered to help with their jumble sale, still raising money for roof. Jill says I have got to go to NADFAS next week (talk on Sèvres porcelain), also put name down for trip to Art Deco exhibition at V&A. Back home, galvanised Alice to chuck out some of her old clothes/CDs/makeup to make way for newly arrived Christmas presents/sale buys so will hardly need to collect much other jumble.

Also spent time replying to e-mails re: website, telling them it's all in hand, respite owing to festive season. Felt like telling them the real reason, that'd shut them up (well, till the gossip started, anyway). Tried to compose suitably sarcastic reply to Derek Fletcher, that man is poison.

Tuesday 14th January

2 p.m. Way forward with website virtually taken out of my hands. Met Ruth at shop, had little moan about amount of work it is (was on it all yesterday, amending) when Usha arrived, promptly posited village website. Feebly forced to admit Debbie had already suggested something similar, but Usha – if I needed a solicitor I know where I'd go (though sadly she doesn't do divorce) – was taking no prisoners and the next thing I knew I'd agreed to hold a meeting about it here tonight.

This much I do know: since Joe Grundy, keen user of Jolene's new 'cyber café' at The Bull (it's come a long way since the days of the bowling green and the Playbar) is bound to come, am not knocking myself out making sandwiches so he can complain about the fillings. After all that fuss about the food at the website launch, he can have bought biscuits and lump it!

10 p.m. Very successful evening. More than a quorum – me, Mum, Usha, Ruth, George, Joe and Jolene – no Lynda, thank goodness, but she'll doubtless hear soon enough. We've decided to form a committee to decide on content, but can already see how it could work: we'll keep the 'Archive' material but can also use the site as sort of village noticeboard, list amenities, publicise forthcoming events, fête, Flower and Produce, etc.

One sour note: Joe Grundy complaining about bought biscuits, said I was 'letting things slide'! And he brought up again (not literally) what he calls the 'prawn things' at the launch. As George succinctly put it, Joe'd cause bother in an empty house.

Next website meeting's been set for Sunday evening, here. Seriously considering suggesting everyone brings their own food, as at Jubilee parties.

Thursday 16th January

Worried about Debbie. Really thought her time away would have bucked her up, but she still seems to be slogging through each day without any motivation or enjoyment. Spoke to Brian about it, which is progress – wouldn't have done so last week. He can see the problem, but feels as he's the prime cause of it, not much he can do. Not very pleasant for him working alongside her, either, I don't suppose. Lambing tailing off now, so perhaps she can take things a bit easier, get out and pick up the threads. Not sure who with, though, since not speaking to Elizabeth and has sworn never to again.

Parallel lives approach with Brian seems to be helping, at any rate. We're still very careful about what we say to each other, but can at least be civil.

Consequently temperature in house has risen above glacial for first time since Christmas.

Friday 17th January

Huge row with Alice this evening – went in to collect her washing, found her prancing about in front of mirror trying on tops for party, complete with pierced belly button. She's had it weeks, apparently, a crowd of them went and had them done after school. Silly, silly girl! Even Kate was over 16 when she had her first piercing. Went off at the deep end a bit, forbade her from going to party, so she's spent rest of evening in room, sulking.

It took Brian to calm me down: pointed out it hadn't gone septic so far, she was obviously looking after it all right, and at least, unlike tattoo, easily undone if she gets bored with it, as she probably will. Realise this is exactly sort of instance where he and I complement each other – or, rather, he grounds me before I get too stratospheric. Made me reflect briefly that if it did ever come to splitting up, life on my own, one-to-one with Alice, would not be easy.

This repairing, though, not easy either. Tried talking to Mum about it, but find it hard to put into words. Despite semblance of 'normal life', still feels totally unnatural, Brian and I actors in a play or something. But at least still some kind of double act.

Sunday 19th January

Nolly's second birthday. Wonderful, wonderful news, best I could have hoped for – Adam's coming home! Not quite sure when, yet, sometime in March he thinks, there's lots of places he still wants to see before he leaves Africa, but just to think I'll see him... especially now with everything that's happened. It's like a dream.

Suddenly everything seems less of a problem. Lynda Snell (here for website meeting) and her 'cascading sheets' of information (pretended to know what she was talking about but must ask Alice), Debbie's being so miserable (if anyone can snap her out of it, Adam can), even things with Brian.

Adam knows about all that: Debbie e-mailed him. Not sure if I mind – in a way I feel it's my secret, but realise she was only trying to protect me. Though she's the one who needs protecting. She's so cold, closed off. As if she's taking out on Brian all her hurt and anger about Simon. And to be honest, she seems to be getting worse, not better.

Adam's news such a bonus because had been starting to feel sorry for myself again. Not surprising, really, had attacked this website thing with all my energy, when should have realised I'm pretty much running on empty and should have rationed myself a bit better. Still not sleeping. That's when I play my favourite memory game – not just all the times Brian was short with me over the past year, and how I stupidly missed the subtext, but, even worse, the nice times which I foolishly thought proved what a good, strong relationship we still had.

There was this one time – early June, I think. Anyway, it was a beautiful evening, calm and still, and he suddenly announced he fancied an evening fishing. And it was so lovely, I went out to find him, and sat on the bank for a bit, among all the buttercups. Then, when I said I'd better go, he suddenly said, as if he really meant it, 'Don't go, Jenny. Please stay.'

And so I did. Didn't think any more of it at the time, of course, except that it was one of those perfect little lulls in life when conversation wasn't necessary, it was just good to be together. And now – well, now I know what was really going on. How a week or so before, the night of our anniversary party – irony of ironies – she'd thought she was miscarrying. She couldn't get hold of Brian, of course, so she rang Tim and he went round and stayed with her, but he was so outraged that next day he drove up here and punched Brian in the yard, hence the black eye. Some farm accident that was! What hydraulic hose? And to think I was so worried!

It'd be so easy if I could just say 'bastard' and write him off. But in truth I don't know what to think. In my good moments I think times like that one by the Am show how torn he was, and that he really did love me all along, he never stopped, and all that stuff he said at Christmas about loving me wasn't just to save his skin. But in my bad ones, I just think: what a bloody hypocrite. How could he live with himself?

Tuesday 21st January

Brian very odd at lunch, probing as to why Adam's coming home. Resolve to be pleasant weakening a bit – Adam's been away for over ten years, isn't that reason enough? Shows how insecure Brian feels, I suppose, but it's as if he thinks Adam's return is some kind of conspiracy, someone else to gang up on him. Ridiculous, not as though I've asked Debbie to behave like she is towards him. Am not going to let on to Brian that Adam knows. Why should I? Let him sweat.

Debbie has done her affidavit for the divorce.

Thursday 23rd January

Received Mum's minutes of website meeting, very efficiently typed up and distributed as hard copy! Something of an irony to have village website secretary who can't/won't use e-mail. Have tried to encourage her to try on my computer, but she seems petrified. Joe and George, meanwhile, going great guns on the computers at The Bull, even Bert Fry has e-mailed me some of his dreadful doggerel which he seems to think deserves a wider audience. Jolene is doing a 'Leisure' page which we all know will consist principally of forthcoming attractions at the pub, but, to be fair, she's also given space to the Playgroup Sponsored Toddle and the next WI meeting. Lynda, meanwhile, is inundating me with material – she was supposed to be doing an edited version of the parish magazine but seems to have taken it upon herself to widen her brief somewhat. No surprises there.

Sunday 26th January

Unseasonably warm, some place in Scotland basking in the 60s apparently. Went round to Brookfield, Pip and Josh engaged on RSPB Garden Birdwatch, very sweet, Phil and Jill there too, also Heather, who came for Christmas and hasn't yet gone home. Maybe she won't, too painful without Solly? There was another happy marriage.

Made me feel a bit miserable. Couldn't help wondering if Brian had been calling Siobhan while I was out. I know we said no contact, but maybe he's taken that as no physical contact and as she's moved away...? Can't ask, don't dare. If I do and he has to admit he is phoning and e-mailing, what then? More rows, more ultimatums. Just don't want it at the moment. Am still picking up bits of self from all over place and trying to reassemble them in some sort of order. Do not want to be blown apart again.

Jennifer's Diary

Monday 27th January

Much hilarity in village over Joe's 'Country Jottings' for the website. Trying to send to me, he appears to have sent them to everyone on The Bull's address list and, being Joe, they were full of howlers e.g. to look out for 'wild privates' in the hedgerows (assume he means privet). Even Debbie gave ghost of a smile. Joe round to me in embarrassment, blaming the spell checker. He seems to think that because it has 'spell' in its name it can magically read his mind.

Debbie still very down, though Kenton, whose relationship with Kathy I will never understand, (though frankly, who am I to judge?) seems to be dropping into the cottage on the odd evening and taking her out to cheer her up. I know Jill worries about Kenton, but I'm grateful for anything or anyone that gives Debbie a bit of a lift. I don't seem to be able to manage it. She only becomes half human when Alice is around and is still treating Brian like a leper. Sometimes it's as if it hurts her even to look at him.

Starting to have slight worry that her sheer animosity could tip up what I'm striving for with Brian. Would be something if it was the daughter, not the vengeful wife, who drove him back into his lover's arms. But how to say this to Debbie? Can't. Instead am trying to be nicer to Brian myself. Not very easy though.

If things were really normal between us, we could help each other over Debbie, like we did with Alice and that stupid belly button thing. But since we both know why Debbie's like she is, and I can't exactly take his side on that, it's never going to happen. Had a word with him obliquely about it, he says we've got to give her time, wait for her to get it out of her system. But what, I said, if she wants to go on remembering? He said he's just got to put up with it for as long as it takes.

Then, just when I was starting to feel almost warm towards him, he went all morose, saying something about having managed to alienate all the women who'd once loved him – presume that includes Siobhan! Could have swung for him, self pitying so-and-so. Whose bloody fault is that?

Maybe this just can't work after all. Too much hard feeling all round. Still feel so bitter about what he's put Debbie through, as well as me. OK, I didn't exactly deserve it, but I have to take some responsibility: it was my (bad) judgment that let me marry him, and choose to stay with him. Debbie's had no choice in the matter.

Friday 31st January

Well, the month started badly, so no surprise it's ended on a bit of a low. Seemed to be going better once I made my decision to get on with things, should have realised it was a bit too good to be true. If I know one thing from post-Caroline, it's that it's not a steady graph.

Have felt pretty down this past week. Suppose, however unrealistic, I'd expected instant results from my 'up and at 'em' resolve. Instead seem to have had my own personal dot. com boom and bust.

Hoping February is better.

Saturday 1st February

Hope misplaced. Snow on Thursday turned to black ice by last night. Went out this morning to find one of my wooden Versailles tubs completely collapsed, mess of bulbs and soil – horrid. Tangled, slithery, snake-like leaves of grape hyacinth, sheathed spears of narcissi, early crocus smashed like broken eggs. Felt disproportionately miserable, could have howled like you do when pregnant at photos of abandoned kittens.

These are the bulbs I planted last autumn, before I knew. When I still thought spring would come.

Sunday 2nd February

Snow all gone, now just cold and mud and grey, grey, grey. Went for walk round farm: mud at edge of puddles sculpted like melted chocolate. Am turning into cross between Kilvert and Nigel Slater.

Me in the kitchen at Christmas – not last Christmas obviously!

Have done nothing but brood about things. Think those first couple of days I was in such shock I was almost beyond pain. Then it hurt like hell, but I had to get a grip – the staff party and everything. Then I thought if I could just get through Christmas, I could go quietly mad, but I tried that on my birthday and it didn't really suit me. Then talking to Mum gave me another tack – after all, how had she and Granny P. got through things? Granny P. twice widowed – Mum with Dad all those years? Determination, discipline – and silence. Keep so busy that you push yourself to exhaustion, till there's no energy left to collapse, because that takes effort. And don't let on to anyone. Got to keep reminding myself of this. And that I'm doing what I want – this is what I chose.

Monday 3rd February

Brian, who himself seems to have made a belated New Year resolution to try harder, returned from Farmer's Cash and Carry with new Versailles tub (had diverted via Garden Centre). But just felt bought off. Is that it now? A marriage built on sufferance and sweeteners?

Replanted it anyway.

Wednesday 5th February

Gorgeous day, blizzard, dazzling snow, then dazzling sun. Worked hard on website, committee meeting tomorrow. Felt a bit better.

Thursday 6th February

Website meeting went OK, was on automatic pilot as couldn't sleep last night, took tablet about 1 a.m., then felt vile. Lynda didn't come, so meeting over fairly swiftly, though expect she'll want everything we've decided changed when she gets the minutes, which Mum is still insisting on doing on her old typewriter. She was very sweet with me, though. Still trying not to worry her too much, or to set her any more against Brian, but had to explain why I was so tired, about not sleeping – and why.

Last few days, Brian's really been making an effort, with Debbie and with me. Warming slightly towards him, so much so that spent all yesterday and the day before on clever bit of semantics – or brainwashing, depending how you look at it. By the end of it I'd actually managed to persuade myself that he hadn't, in fact, been lying to me all last year. All he'd done was to conceal something, and that was actually something quite different. And, what's more, that in concealing things from me, he was actually trying to protect me, protect us and our marriage. He'd done it because he really did care about me and he didn't want things to change. In fact it was him showing that he loved me.

Warped or what, I now think, because having gone to bed all consoled, started thinking about Debbie, and how Brian loved her too. How good he'd been over that business with Simon. About Honeysuckle. And how he'd offered money towards buying it for them. Suddenly struck me. Well, of course he did! It was putting money – our money – in Siobhan's pocket!

It's sick. Sick. But at the same time...

Brian looks dreadful. Really haggard. Debbie still not speaking to him in any real sense. He and I moving in separate orbits. The farm going through a tough time. Yet for this he gave up his mistress and his son.

Mum says I'm crazy. He doesn't deserve thinking about, let alone sympathy. But it's not just him I'm thinking about, it's Ruairi, and even Siobhan, on her own with the baby, and no father around.

It's all such a mess. Maybe I should have let her have him. Can't see how being on my own would hurt any more than this. And at least someone could be happy out of it.

Mum tried to be soothing, obviously at a loss, bless her. Said we had to give it time (yes, yes). And that maybe Brian and I should get away for a few days, perhaps when Alice is skiing at half term.

To be honest, the prospect of time away with him horrifies me. What if we found that without the crutch of our daily routine, the whole thing collapsed?? And I'd be terrified he'd be comparing it with the times he had with her, which just haunt me. Can't get Biarritz out of my head, imagining them strolling around, eating out, everyone thinking they were a couple. Going back to the room, in bed together... When she was, what, six months pregnant? He was never that interested in me when I was pregnant. It just upsets me too much to think about.

Saturday 8th February

Back to being angry today. Anger's better, I can achieve things when I'm angry. Among other things, fired off curt e-mail to Derek Fletcher who complained new picture of Grey Gables golf course had him in it without his permission. Had to look twice before I could see him, he is in distance, but obviously stuck in a bunker.

Reason for anger is Debbie doing the accounts, IACS, etc., and profits are well down. She won't usually mention Brian's name, but said something unguarded over coffee about how we'd be making more profit if not for his 'bizarre' lifestyle.

Take it she means the maintenance payments for Ruairi. Have never asked how much they are but once started to think, imagine quite generous. Suppose they are Siobhan's only income, till Honeysuckle sells (though it's apparently under offer). The more I think about it, the more I'm sure Brian must be paying handsomely. And to think how he goes on about my spending, threatens to cut up my Underwoods card, etc., etc! Very glad now Alice is going on school ski trip, had said no to new anorak, hat, goggles etc., but have told her we are going to Birmingham this afternoon to kit her out, all new stuff from head to toe, O'Neill, Quiksilver, she can have what she likes.

He breaks my heart so I break the bank. Trite, but true.

Sunday 9th February

Trip to Birmingham rather mixed – great success for Alice, awful for me. OK in ski shop, but every other shop bursting with obscene crimson hearts and fluffy teddies for Valentine's Day. Alice wanted to look at everything, bought heart-shaped lollipop for particular boy she likes and why wasn't I getting a card for Brian? Nightmare. My punishment for plotting such a petty revenge.

Monday 10th February

Maybe it was latent threat of Valentine's Day that's made this month so difficult all along – stupid what an unconscious pressure these things are. Alice agitating about the cards she's sending, getting Debbie to write the envelopes, and when best to post them so they arrive on the day, but will post come before said boys leave for school? Just thankful she's not sending one to Will Grundy (or Ed!), though maybe has simply had sense not to show me. Poor Debbie obviously gritting her teeth as well.

Wednesday 12th February

Horrors, Brian asked today if I'd like to do anything special on Friday! Had to pretend hadn't realised what day it was, was suitably vague. Idea of time away together, romantic candlelit dinner appals. Going to tell him we should ignore it, just treat it as normal day.

He tried to talk to Debbie about things today, says she gave him short shrift. Suppose I should give him some credit for trying.

Thursday 13th February

In village, Tony pointed out tread on one of my tyres is worn, amusingly quipped was Brian trying to get rid of me? Getting it changed tomorrow.

Friday 14th February

While Brian was out doing my tyre, van arrived from posh modern florist in Oriel Road and unloaded beautiful hand-tied bouquet. Looked and smelt divine. Brian came back, covered in confusion, said he'd ordered them before I said 'let's ignore it' and couldn't catch van to stop them. Very proud of self as managed only split-second mental flash of 'I wonder how many times he bought her flowers there?' before saying dignified thank you.

At least he had sense not to send red roses.

Saturday 15th February

Alice off skiing, coach from school at crack of dawn. House very quiet without her. Seems that without even trying Brian and I have got time on our own together after all, though at least can hide in respective studies if we have to. We shall see.

Friday 21st February

Looking forward to Alice coming home. This week hasn't gone quite as I imagined – not quite sure what I imagined, but it wasn't the one we've had, mostly characterised by awkward silences. My fault, mostly. Brian still trying so hard, with both me and Debbie, and not getting much back, from either of us. Can't help myself, though. Despite determination earlier in year, find it so hard to make self move towards him. And Debbie's gone very strange. Keeps floating off with Kenton, then announced she's taking tomorrow morning off to go shopping. Debbie, shopping! Worst thing is, Brian just sits there and takes it, says he'll cover. It's so not like her – not like either of them. Makes me long for the old days, when they cared enough – about the farm, about each other – to argue. Now it's like there's nothing left, and if there isn't, what's the point?

Fed up with feeling so depressed. Mum says maybe things'll be better when Adam comes home. Hope so – though it seems hard on him. Even though he knows how things are, he can't really appreciate what he's coming back to. Doesn't seem very fair, somehow.

Saturday 22nd February

Counting the hours till Alice gets back, poor love. As if she wants her pathetic mother smothering her the minute she gets off the coach. She'll probably be exhausted.

This week has been salutary lesson in what the house might be like one day, if we make it that far, when Alice has left home and it's just Brian and me rattling around. Scary. Keep trying to tell myself that, with the revolving door policy that seems to operate here, Adam might still be around, or Phoebe have come to live with us, or something. Not quite sure why either of these things might happen, but slightly saner than my other fantasy, where Siobhan dies somehow and we take on Ruairi...

Well, it would give Brian and me something to do, some reason for staying together. I'm hard put to find another at the moment.

Sunday 23rd February

Alice back precisely ten hours, am already wishing her away again. She is playing a new CD non-stop, including a track which laments piteously something about looking pretty happy in their family portrait and wanting to go back to it. If only.

Monday 24th February

Am definitely going mad. Bring up Ruairi? What about Siobhan's vast extended family? Surely they'd all rally round? And even more bizarre, with Adam due back any day... isn't that exactly what Paddy and Nora wanted to do with him?

Part of the huge pain of all this has been digging up so many other, buried memories. And let's face it, not just Brian's love life. I'm not entirely blameless when it comes to affairs. I haven't exactly got both feet firmly on the moral high ground.

It crucifies me now to think about me and Paddy. Not the short timespan of our affair, not the remembered sweetness of it, but how I could have done what I did to Nora. She was engaged to him, for heaven's sake, and I never gave her a thought. Just took his line that they both knew what was what, that things weren't good between them. All the time I was seeing him on the quiet, she was working at The Bull, pouring pints, wiping the bar – and I was sloping off to see him, made up to the nines, sweeping through from the back like Lady Muck. What must have been going through her head? I can imagine, now, all too well,

117

but I didn't then. You box it off, don't you, your guilt? You don't see what doesn't put you in a good light.

But their engagement must still have meant something – to her, a hell of a lot – for them to come up with the idea of adopting Adam. What on earth was all that about? A way of neutering any threat from me? Is that how Siobhan would have seen my idea for Brian to see Ruairi, with me in tow? It's dizzying, to keep jumping the fence like this. But I have been on both sides. I ought to remember that sometimes when I'm being hard on Brian.

March a week away and still no word from Adam about when he might be home. Alice says England is 'boring', can't understand why he wants to come back at all. She loved her skiing, wants us all to go at Christmas. Christmas!

Friday 28th February

Still nothing from Adam. Feeling increasingly desperate. Decorators finished his room yesterday, am very pleased, think he'll like it. Quite plain, but restful – duck-egg blue walls and new bed linen in almost a Tattersall check. Moved furniture back today, Brian helping, though he will keep asking why Adam's coming home and how long he'll be staying. He's obviously terrified Adam will become someone else to gang up on him. Am quite intrigued myself to know how Adam will react. He's been away so long, feel we all have to get to know him all over again.

Saturday 1st March

Keep trying Adam's mobile, no reply, only message service, could be switched off or out of range. Have e-mailed every address I've ever had for him, to no avail. Where is he?

Monday 3rd March

Adam back!! Walked into kitchen at lunchtime to find him and Debbie sitting there having coffee!! Silly thing had got a last-minute flight, came all the way from Heathrow to Hollerton via goodness knows how many connections, and Debbie met him there. Tried to say we could have picked him up at airport, he wouldn't have any of it, says if ten years in Third World haven't prepared him for vagaries of Virgin trains (all new to him of course, it was British Rail when he left), nothing will.

Could have hugged him all day. Looks thin, but well, tanned of course. Apart from that, same old Adam. Paddy's fabulous eyes. He was darling to me, said I looked fantastic considering all that's been going on, how could Brian... etc., etc. Told him that we are trying to save the marriage (are we?), really want to work at it (do we?) and could he just please go along with it for now. He said he'd try. Perhaps I'll feel a bit more like trying myself now he's home. So happy. Love him to bits.

Monday 10th March

Adam home a week now and the difference is palpable. No time to write before because house has been stream of visitors, all keen to see the Prodigal Son – and he's worth the visit. All right, I'm biased, but he's simply gorgeous: not just good-looking but so considerate, clever, funny... also – hardly surprising, I suppose – seems so worldly. Found him giving me advice today on mending things with Brian (said it might be like a broken leg: stronger in the end provided given enough time and opportunity to heal). Also, to my amazement, he's managed to get Brian to talk to him. Told me the things Brian's not able to: how sorry Brian. is, what a mess he made of things, how very much he loves me. Said he was very humble.

Feel bad, as if I'm using Adam as conduit between me and Brian: we ought to be talking about these things face to face, the two of us. But Brian's not good at emotion and I know with me, the hurt is still so deep that if we did, it'd only go wrong and boil over into tears or anger. Best to wait.

Asked Adam how he was so wise: implied – well, as good as said – he'd had his heart broken. Feel sure this is why, deep down, he's come home. And a lot of support we are! But when said this, he said it had been over for some time, travelling round Africa had been to get it out of his system. Said, anyway, there comes a point when other people's problems are more interesting than your own: that, in fact, is when you know you're over it. Can't wait.

Even Adam, though, hasn't been able to get Debbie to open up. She's still so icy, so distant with Brian. Will barely discuss the farm, won't sit down to a meal with him or anything. Trod same old ground: double betrayal, bottling everything up, denial as way of coping. I also said felt she despised me for taking Brian back when she'd had courage to throw Simon out. though after talking through with Adam, I now wonder if even deeper down she's jealous because Brian was willing to come back whereas Simon simply cleared off.

Friday 14th March

Brian out at CLA lunch. (Still spot-checking and this one, at least, is for real. Suppose, logically, three hours out of house not really time enough for flight there and back to Dublin, plus torrid meeting with her and tearful reunion with Ruairi, but whoever said insane mistrust, fear and jealousy were logical?) Adam suggested he, Debbie and I had lunch together, 'just like old times', etc., etc., and we were just howling at some story of Adam's (yes, Debbie too) when Brian got back. Asked what we were laughing at, and – well, it had been a long story, impossible either to retell or to summarise. Atmosphere instantly flat, Debbie excused herself, then Adam. Poor Brian left standing there. Felt desperate for him – and stupid. What do I keep saying? That I have to try. That he has to feel there's something worth staying for. Otherwise what earthly reason has he got to be here? Offered olive-branch coffee. He said no thanks, going for walk. We are hopeless.

Tuesday 18th March

Thank God. Brian and I have finally had the conversation we should have had weeks, months ago – and initiated by him, which I think, in a perverse way, was what I actually wanted. Though had expected it to come from me, in the end perhaps it has to be the transgressor who makes the move.

He's basically said what I know: I have to 'cut him a bit of slack' was how he put it. (Conversation came about because I snapped at him in front of David.) B. says he feels as though he's banging his head against a wall, even Alice now being infected/affected by atmosphere and starting to ignore him. Denied it, but know it's true. Told him again did want to make a go of things, but that find it hard, harder than I could have imagined.

Couldn't say this is because sometimes feel so tired/old/pathetic and yet know have only self to blame for shape life has taken. I could, after all, have stayed a single mother. I didn't have to marry Brian – or Roger, for that matter, after horrible failure of which, married Brian effectively on the rebound. It's far too easy to blame all our ills on Brian's philandering when know I brought with me a thoroughly confused mindset, muddled expectations and an entire removal van of baggage. Oh, and two children, of course. One of whom has had to go to Africa to get his heart comprehensively broken – make his mistakes well away from home, perhaps, having been expected to be too perfect here, too much my surrogate husband in between real ones? And Debbie: easy to blame her two imperfect fathers for her attraction to Simon, the older man/father figure who turned out to be an eternal child. But in a way, perhaps she recognised that about him – it was what she wanted, what she knew. Because hasn't she always been the one who's had to mother me?

Friday 21st March

Astonishing day. Suddenly, without expecting it, feel so much has shifted. After three solid months of dither, feel total relief. Brian is back in control.

First, at breakfast, announced he is buying Alice a new horse. No conditions attached, no 'ifs' and 'buts', no 'wait till your birthday' or 'do well in your exams'. Said he can see Chandler is too small, doesn't matter whether she's serious about riding or not, even if simply for pleasure, she needs a bigger horse. Alice over the moon. On the one hand, can see it's a strategy – win round the floating voter, as it were – but at the same time can't help admiring him for doing something to shake the inertia, to move us all on.

Mum round for coffee and told her about it. When Brian came in, found myself half-teasing him, just like we used to – and in front of Mum! – me saying it was blatant attempt to curry favour, he saying he had to cultivate the one member of the family who still loved him. A month, a week ago, days ago even, there'd have been an undertone, but today we got away with it. Felt such triumph. Suddenly, without trying, there was the 'normality' I simply hadn't been able to remember how to do. Then we just chit-chatted about Mum's triumph in finally sending an e-mail. Brian said something about at least knowing it was possible now, and having the confidence to persevere. And then he gave me a sort of conspiratorial look, and I realised he hadn't been talking about the e-mail at all. It gave me a real wobble, and I remembered some of why I fell in love with him, and why I've gone on loving him: the cleverness, the quick-wittedness, the subtlety. Not just rare in a farmer. Rare in anyone.

Then, if that wasn't enough, this afternoon took flask of tea out to lambing shed, expecting Adam, but had gone to the gym. And Brian sort of squared up and told me straight, about something that happened yesterday.

Before Siobhan left, apparently, for some reason he agreed to pay to get her stuff shipped over to Ireland. Anyway, the lease on the flat's expired, so Elizabeth had packed it all up and yesterday brought the invoice round so Brian could give her a cheque. The way he told it, it was purely a business arrangement, and at least he was telling me, albeit after the event. But – ghastly – it seems Debbie walked in as he was handing over the cheque, and absolutely flipped. Called Elizabeth all sorts of names, then called Brian all sorts of names, all the same stuff, deceit, betrayal,

Siobhan still in his life – which he hotly denies.

The cynic in me – the cynic of a month/week/days ago – would be asking why he didn't tell me last night, instead of now when I was nicely softened up by offer of horse for Alice – but I don't see it like that any more. And he almost didn't seem so worried for himself, anyway, as worried for Debbie, that she's gone beyond just suppressing rage and now is actually damaging herself. And (and this from Brian, who regards counsellors as the Anti-Christ) that she needs help which we can't give her because she won't admit to us that there's anything wrong.

The last thing I'd want is for Debbie's problems to be a way out of ours, but can't help feeling that in her we have something real to bind us together – better than any amount of pretend 'normality' like going out to dinner or taking a few days away – even, than him carrying on running the farm and me doing the website. Perhaps the very difficulty of dealing with her will be the thing that pulls us round.

First day of spring. First day of lots of things, perhaps.

Sunday 23rd March

Trying not to get ground down by doomy feeling which is prevailing in Sunday papers that this war with Iraq, which started four days ago with bombing campaign of so-called 'shock and awe', is going badly and could drag on. Don't want anything to dent my new optimism, but things do seem bad. Debbie depressed by whole thing, she says, Alice wishes she had been here and not on ski trip to go on 'Stop the War' march (glad she wasn't), Adam has old school friend in Army out there. Grim.

Doesn't seem right time to talk to Debbie about seeing a counsellor. Just feel it might push her away even more, as if we were writing her off, unable to help her ourselves, or couldn't be bothered with her any more.

Tuesday 25th March

It's official: Brian is the best dad in the world, at least according to Alice, who is soon, once Alistair has vetted him, to be the proud new owner of the very beautiful Spearmint, 15.2, nine-year-old bay gelding. All being well, he's arriving on Sunday.

And a nice surprise: the children have decided to cook me lunch for Mothering Sunday – a course each. As Alice can only, to my knowledge, cook scrambled eggs (occasionally successful), chocolate chip cookies (usually raw in middle) and mess of pasta which she calls a bake (needs work on presentation) and Debbie also not known for skill in kitchen, am intrigued as to what I may expect. Brian very discreetly/sweetly suggested he spend day in lambing shed, obviously trying to avert a Debbie confrontation, but feel it's time we made a statement that he is to be included, whether she likes it or not, so told Brian I would positively like him to be there. He seemed genuinely pleased.

Sunday 30th March

Extraordinary lunch – tomato and mozzarella salad (Alice); lamb curry (Adam) and apple crumble (Debbie) – could I suppose be termed international fusion food? Was to have been carrot and coriander soup to start but timings thrown, indeed Alice's entire participation in doubt, owing to arrival mid-morning of Spearmint, who naturally had to be cosied into his lovingly-prepared stable, shown hay net, water, etc., etc., and generally fussed. The minute lunch was over (Debbie mercifully silent throughout),

Alice dragged her off to coo over him again. Only Kate missing, and even she'd phoned, so cup (and stomach) truly full, more so when Brian paid me the best – at the moment, to be fair, the only safe – compliment he could. Said I am a fantastic mother. Not so sure, but good to hear it anyway.

Tuesday 1st April

April Fool's Day: Debbie received decree nisi. Only heard this from Adam, who has taken on role of counsellor as we all (me, him and Brian) agree that realistically our chances of getting Debbie to go for any kind of paid-for therapy are nil. He tried to get her to let it all out, but still she won't.

Feel very cowardly for not being more proactive with Debbie myself, but honestly think she's better off with Adam. I'm the wrong person to help her. Don't know even how I have the nerve to think I could when can't help feeling I've caused so many of her problems. All very well to blame her inadequate/absent fathers, but just too easy. Surely the person who was around has got to take some of the responsibility too?

Wednesday 2nd April

Initially deceptive e-mail from Derek Fletcher praising my 'charming' website piece on Mothering Sunday, past and present, before launching into tirade against feckless single parents. Thanks, Derek!

Saturday 5th April

Even in Africa, Adam says, where traditionally certain women past or incapable of childbearing are compensated with near-mythological status and accredited with having special powers, they'd be hard put to accommodate Lynda Snell. For his 60th birthday, she's only given Robert two llamas who rejoice in the names of Wolfgang and Constanza. (She did explain but the connection escapes me – can Mozart's wife really have been South American – earlier incarnation of Mick and Bianca Jagger? Surely not.) These she has installed in her paddock, though apparently they won't be confined there for long, as she plans to walk them about on halters and, in time, harness them to a cart. Truly bizarre.

Equally bizarre, Kenton round on the scrounge for paint – not that we had any, am hanging on to rest of Adam's duck-egg blue, may re-do downstairs loo. Anyway, having persuaded Jack (a) to buy Daphne's Caff in Borchester and (b) to make him (Kenton) manager, he's got to do up the flat above it, Daphne's Den, as he calls it, where she has nonchalantly chain-smoked beneath polystyrene ceiling tiles for the past forty years, never opening a window. Still, he seems thrilled at the prospect. And I know Phil and Jill are relieved he's finally found something not too nefarious (think their worst moment was when he was thinking of managing a lap-dancing club). Poor Jill. Even Kate never pushed me that far.

Also bizarre, though intriguingly so, Brian says I am to keep Monday free, he has a surprise for me. Says I've been looking tired, and am not to work so hard on website. Can't help liking it when he tells me what to do. Both relaxing and delicious.

Monday 7th April

7 p.m. It was the Antiques Fair! I know he's making an effort, but for Brian to give up a day (a lovely day, too, diamond-bright sunshine) to wander round fusty old Felpersham Town Hall looking at willow pattern plates and hunting prints really is quite something. I absolutely hadn't guessed; when he said 'day out' I'd assumed a day at a deer farm or

something – but he insisted it was my treat, it was about me enjoying myself. Pointed out that assumption of deer farm trip wasn't quite so off-the-mark – we did after all spend our honeymoon touring farms.

Over lunch – fancy new wine bar, all ox-blood leather sofas and arresting oil paintings – had little memory-jogging session about how hot it was that summer ('76) and why we went to Cambridgeshire, of all places, on our honeymoon. How he'd been thinking at the time of going in for Brussels sprouts. (Glad he didn't, can imagine what Alice would have to say about living on a sprout farm, especially if we had sprout acreage where riding course is now.) How he'd wanted to look up old friends, to show me off, he said. The lovely places we stayed – pastel-washed brick-and-timber inns bowed down with rambler roses. And how Brian had always booked the best room, bridal suite, four-poster, half-tester – even, in one place, a cherrywood sledge-bed. How there was always chilled champagne waiting when we got there with dry throats and dusty shoes, and how we'd open it and dive together into the bath, into bed, not necessarily in that order... The sledge-bed had a raspberry damask cover. I can feel it now, cool and slippery against my sunburnt shoulders. And Brian warm against me. Didn't say any of this last bit to him, of course. Can't expose myself that much just yet.

Pottered around Antiques Fair all afternoon, looking at things, picking them up, putting them down, Brian not once complaining about being tired or bored. For once felt no impulse to buy. In car on way home, he put on 'Madame Butterfly'. Brian's not a great one for symbolic gestures, but – girl wins boy, girl loses boy, girl kills herself? Well, I'm not dead, nor about to be, so Cio-Cio-San's got to be Siobhan, surely? Substituting self-imposed exile in Ireland for the suicide? Fanciful, I know, but after

128

such a lovely day felt could allow myself to be.

Brian, teasing, said he was amazed we'd had such a good time without me spending any money, but this time did tell him what I feel – which is that today wasn't about spending money, more about him noticing me, noticing I was tired and doing something about it – something I'd like – and which he wouldn't, much. Also thanked him properly for buying Spearmint for Alice. And for working so hard on the farm lately. Because what it means for me is a shoring up of everything we have, working to consolidate what he can, even if our emotional foundations are still too shaky to start reconstructing anything.

'Un Bel Di' – well, we had had a fine day. And perhaps – just perhaps – we're going to be all right.

Tuesday 8th April

Ironic I should have thought we might be going to deer farm yesterday, as today Adam was asking Brian about other deer producers in area. On quiet, he told me he's surprised Brian's prepared to sell deer as we do, taking market price on the day, when could get much higher return with some kind of direct marketing, e.g. farmers markets. He's tried the idea out on Debbie but she was very negative, says Brian won't be interested. Also very bitter about Spearmint and even my day out, saying Brian's trying to buy us off, it's divide and rule. Can't bear it for her – her whole outlook on life seems so twisted. Adam agrees. He's still doing his best to take her out of herself, but she flatly refuses to go out with him and this crowd he's met through the gym.

Mum round for tea. Told her what a boon Adam's being, to all of us, and that main obstacle to Brian's and my reconciliation seems to be Debbie, though at least we've recognised this and are trying to work round it. Mum and I agreed she's not going to talk about it, it's not her way. Trouble is, am not really sure what is.

Wednesday 9th April

War in Iraq seems to be over as soon as it began. As statue of Saddam Hussein in downtown Baghdad toppled, onlookers cheered and began pelting it with shoes (sign of deep disrespect apparently). Extraordinary moment – you could practically hear Rageh Omaar jumping up and down with excitement (poor thing probably can't wait to get back to Johannesburg to wife and babies – he reminds me of so much of Lucas). End seems more than slightly anti-climactic, but everyone seems agreed it is over, if nothing else because extraordinary Iraqi Minister of Information – with his astonishing daily assertions that Saddam was still in control when you could see occupying Americans lounging in back of shot – seems to have called it a day.

Friday 11th April

Adam's persuaded Brian to at least let him have a look at different ways of marketing the deer – quite a breakthrough! Know this is another concession to me on Brian's part, he's normally so defensive about the farm, won't admit any alternative, but he's given Adam the go-ahead to research what the mark-up would be from direct selling, be it mail-order, farmers markets, local health-food shops, whatever. Feel ridiculously excited about it. Reminded Brian of when we first got the deer and tried to butcher one on the kitchen table – this was before all the health regulations they've brought in – God, the mess! – but it was fun, in a way, something new we were doing together. And if Adam's idea does go somewhere, well, it'll be another new direction for Home Farm which, truthfully, Hungary aside, since all the flurry of diversification – riding course, fishing lake – has been standing still these last ten years. (And we all know that when Brian stands still, his eye starts to wander.) Brian rather gruff, pretending he'd only OK'd Adam's initiative because, with all the talk of decoupling, we could lose a lot in subsidy, so may as well start maximising the return on the deer now and get ahead of the game.

Not only that, but he's getting Adam a car, to be paid for by Brian not changing his own this year. This may not sound much from a man who's already driving a top-of-the-range Mercedes, but the brochures about the new model have been in the sitting room since Christmas, and I know Oliver Sterling's having one. Anyway, Brian says it's not much of a sacrifice, Adam has earned it, after all he's not taking a salary and, assuming he stays over the summer, will be saving us the cost of a student.

Debbie and Alice went for a ride, then pasta at cottage. Adam out to eat, then on to a club in Felpersham with these new friends, so it was just Brian and me for supper. Had got beautiful turbot, just did it very simply, how Brian likes it, en paupiette with wine and herbs. Bottle of Pouilly Fuissé. Afterwards, he made coffee, I went and collapsed on sofa. When he came in with tray, let him pour, swung feet down for him to sit down, then automatically swung them back up again into his lap, just like I always have – well, used to. He seemed a bit surprised – not as surprised as I was! But stayed like it anyway.

Jennifer's Diary

Saturday 12th April

Excitement hotting up in village over forthcoming 'Ambridge Three Peaks Challenge' (Heydon Berrow, Lakey Hill and tower of St Stephen's, would you believe), which David and Alistair have dreamed up as a church fund-raiser for Easter Monday. Alice has persuaded Adam to enter (or was it the other way round? You can never tell with those two, not sure who's the bigger child at heart). Now only debate on costumes remains: Adam suggested pantomime horse as she's so horse-mad, but Alice has vetoed that as would slow them down too much. So now they're on to Plan B, which they are keeping as closely guarded a secret as Lynda Snell's costume, which she has promised is something very, very special. Adam tried to jolly Debbie into entering with them, of course she was having none of it.

Another two weeks have gone by with no improvement in her. Cannot just go on believing it will cure itself in time (what she says she's doing) or ignoring it (exactly what she is doing). It's been nearly six months now since Simon. Am seriously wondering if shouldn't try to get her to see a doctor. Desperately guilty as know I've put myself and my needs (Brian) before hers. Not something that mothers are supposed to do, but sheer self-preservation. But in preserving my sense of worth, have I destroyed hers?

Sunday 13th April

Palm Sunday. Nonsensical scenes at church during donkey procession. Lynda's llamas, which she'd brought along (don't ask), so spooked by sight of donkey that they sat down plumb in the middle of the path as we were winding our way round churchyard. Refused to budge. After several wasted minutes, procession had to be re-routed round the back, past the compost heap and the bins.

Adam on internet all afternoon, sussing out other venison producers in area. Says there aren't many, thinks he has uncovered real gap in market. He and Brian are going to Hollerton farmers market on Tuesday to see what it's like. Debbie in briefly at tea time to arrange a ride with Alice. Looks dreadful. Says she thinks she's going down with something. Hoped this might be good excuse to get her to doctor, she said it's probably viral and they wouldn't give her anything anyway, then stomped off to do some top-dressing. She has an answer for everything.

Tuesday 15th April

Very successful day – well, from Adam's point of view at least. Though Brian put up token resistance about start-up costs, Adam says these are minimal and is sure we could make a go of it. No other venison producer at market, so a definite gap. No need to ask who'd end up actually standing behind the stall, but to tell the truth, I wouldn't mind at all. I'd like to be a bit more involved, it'd make a welcome change from the website, and collecting the fees for the riding course and fishing lake hardly feels like making much of a contribution. Adam and Debbie too busy on farm itself of course, but Alice could help in school holidays. Brian says anyone but him. Flatly refuses to stand around in a stripy apron being nice to the public all day.

Wednesday 16th April

Lynda round, minus llamas, thankfully, but with petition about the Grundys' pole barn. She says it's an illegal structure and a blot on the landscape. Thought she'd have been pleased they'd moved all the clutter there from the verge and their garden, but no. Didn't sign it, used website as tenuous excuse and said I couldn't be seen to take sides. She accepted this reasonably gracefully: seems to have plenty of support from Glebelands people, esp. Fletchers, surprise, surprise.

Debbie looking very pale and admits to headache/shivers. Still determined not to go to doctor, says she'll only catch something in waiting room as it will be full of people with slight sore throat panicking they've got SARS.

Thursday 17th April

2 p.m. At last! Debbie came into work this morning but within an hour had to admit defeat and retreated to cottage. Refused all offers to be put to bed in house. Have just been to check on her, take lemon and honey, throat sweets, etc. and she is at least in bed, which is where she should have been since last weekend. Not surprising all this should come out physically at last – she's obviously run-down. Has agreed to let me go down later to take her some soup, and can also use Alice as go-between.

Adam sprayed some mildewed barley which Debbie had missed, so Brian was pleased about that, but he (Brian) has seemed a bit down this week, which has pulled me down a bit as well. We seemed to have been making such progress, but suppose it's not a steady graph for him, either. When Hayley came to collect Phoebe's cardigan the other day, she'd got a sweet little baby with her which she was minding for a friend. Suppose he was about five or six months old. We were standing in the yard chatting when Brian came back and he was really strange around the baby, awkward, but in a clumsy way you could tell he was interested. Have worked out Ruairi was five months on Monday. Brian must miss him like anything.

Friday 18th April

Easter Vigil this afternoon at Penny Hassett, decorating St Stephen's tomorrow. Spent all vigil, when should have been thinking about higher things, thinking about Brian and Siobhan, Ruairi, Debbie, Adam. About time, really – am aware diary seems to have reverted lately to more what it was last year, mix of village trivia and family goings-on. Suppose this must be a good thing: the 'normality' I was after. But things aren't normal really, are they?

It's no wonder Brian's a bit low this week – no wonder Debbie's finally succumbed, either. It doesn't matter whether you're religious or not, at this time of year you can't escape the sense of new beginnings, spring springing, hope rising – supposedly. The gardens are ridiculously prolific – our daffodils are virtually over, but tulips are still everywhere, primroses, bluebells opening already in some places – and the trees are iridescent, dazzling. Miss looking at them for a day and the hedges and orchards are like fast-forwarded film, you can practically see the buds opening. And if you're in the right frame of mind, it's all terribly life-enhancing/Oh to be in England/joys of spring stuff, makes you want to play Elgar at full volume with the windows flung open. But if you're not... it's no coincidence, is it, that it was this time of year Pat succumbed to her depression, and that April's reputedly the worst month for suicides?

Anyway, three hours of enforced quiet gave me a lot of time to think. Started with the children. Started, actually, by counting my blessings – giving thanks for Kate and Alice. Kate, who after all that heart-searching, seems to have settled down the best of any of them, and Alice, love her, a real woman-child, half the time parties, boys and pierced belly buttons, the rest spent grooming Spearmint, fussing Chandler and entering village fancy-dress races — all without any sense of irony. That was a pleasant few minutes, anyway. After that it was all downhill.

Debbie. Poor, darling Debbie. Second child, but first daughter. My Christmas baby, conceived and born within the same year — my love-child with Roger. So like him, the deep-set eyes, the hairline. So like him, even the backs of her knees are his. A child in his own image, but it wasn't enough to keep him, was it? Or I wasn't. Why didn't I fight harder for that marriage? Why didn't I say what I thought? Why did I think that I had to do what he wanted, why did I think that if I was nice and compliant he might be a bit nicer to me? If we'd kept it together, would Debbie be any happier? Would I? Or would it just have meant putting up with Roger's affairs instead of Brian's?

'You can't go back, Mum,' I kept hearing Debbie saying as I sat there, looking at the sun through the side windows and the banner Penny Hassett WI had made for the Millennium. She's so tough, so rational, so practical. No wonder she's always got on so well with Brian. They don't 'do' emotion, either of them. But Debbie hasn't always been like that. How's she taught herself not to feel? And why? Have horrible feeling it's because I've always been so keen to do it for her. That no sooner did she come in from school crying, saying so-and-so had left her out at break, than I'd take over, finishing her sentences, sympathising, suggesting ways round it, or worse, going to see the teacher, making a fuss, when that was the last thing Debbie needed.

All she wanted, probably, was a hug and a chocolate biscuit, then to be left alone with her pony. But it was me, over-compensating madly for my own inadequacies, who made a drama, not even out of a crisis, but out of the everyday. Until she stopped telling me anything at all.

Roger desperately wanted this photo taken though Debbie doesn't look too sure.

And the worst time, when she was 21… when Roger came back. I can hardly bear to think about it. That was her moment, or should have been, her long-lost father coming back to find her. But I stole it, I stole him, it had to be about me, as usual, not about her. Her own father and I couldn't share him with her. And yet she's never reproached me for that, never said a word. (Nor has Brian, though he could have, lately.) But Debbie just buried it. Another emotional landmine.

So yes, I've made my mistakes with Debbie all right. But with Adam I thought I'd done a better job, all in all. And there was one thing I thought I'd really got right – at least one good decision. Till Adam said something the other week – that he had missed not knowing his real father. That there had been something 'missing'. So all that time in Africa was he looking for something, or someone, really? And did he find it? Until he got his heart broken, that is?

So there we are – a daughter who's an emotional ice-block and a son with his emotions a bit too much on the surface? Thankfully the bell started tolling and we were done.

Sunday 20th April

Easter Sunday, and of course can't help thinking back to this day last year, when Brian flew off to Hungary, then was 'delayed' coming back – and I think we can guess where. Brought me perfume and Alice shedloads of airport chocolate to make up for it – nice to know we were worth the bribe. Still, it's no good harking back. Onwards and upwards, etc., despite recent maunderings. Got to get on with things.

Easter lunch not such a big deal as usual as Adam and Alice keen to get out and practise for Three Peaks tomorrow, in costume this time, which has been revealed as Adam in panto horse get-up and Alice in riding gear, whipping him along if he's not careful – she's so competitive, as Brian noted with pride. Took Debbie's lunch down to cottage, she was up, at least, and wrapped in duvet watching old film. Thanked me for emergency food supplies I sneaked in on Friday, not that she'd used much – has no appetite. Won't hear of calling doctor out. Adam had been in to check what needed doing on farm, spraying etc., not that she said she felt she was much use, head like cotton wool. Told her not to worry, Adam had it all in hand. Suspect this was not right thing to say.

Monday 21st April

4 p.m. Alice in furious temper – she and Adam doing really well in Three Peaks when, on arrival at church tower found Lynda Snell in costume – massive jewel-bedecked foam Fabergé egg – blocking staircase. Like umbrella able to go up a chimney but not down, the hoops had wedged her on descent. Fell to Adam to source shears from Glebe and cut her out though before he could swathe her in blanket, emergence at foot of tower captured by 'Echo' photographer. As a result Adam and Alice beaten in the couples section by Susan and Neil Carter, though Home Farm not entirely without glory as Jeff won the solo category. Brian says it just shows Jeff can move fast when he wants to, pity he doesn't demonstrate this ability at work. Hope return of sarcasm means he is back on form.

6 p.m. Have taken Alice over to Stables in bid to improve her temper, Shula is schooling her and Spearmint for Pony Club three-day eventing challenge. She's also keen for her to do more jumping and enter the Pony Club jumping event in May – seems to think Alice shows real potential. Brian reminded me this is exactly what was said about Shula when she was Alice's age and predicts Alice a glittering career in estate agency. Definitely back on form.

Tuesday 22nd April

Think Brian's improved mood may actually have something to do with Debbie being out of the picture. At lunch it transpired that not only has he given Adam go-ahead to continue sussing out farmer's market idea for venison, but is also considering Adam's idea of soft fruit (strawberries). Brian at first feared PYO (could have told Adam that was a non-starter – Brian letting the public swarm all over the farm – I don't think so!) but Adam is thinking bigger scale, i.e. marketing through a co-op. Brian seems really keen, says it's great to have someone with so much enthusiasm around. When Brian had gone out, Adam, bless him, sensitive to Debbie's feelings, says he doesn't want her left out, these aren't to be seen as 'his' ideas. Says he'll tell her about the strawbs when she's better.

Jennifer's Diary

Wednesday 23rd April

Alice off to her three-day eventing looking gorgeous, if nervous, in new jacket. Spearmint very spruce too, has been groomed within an inch of his life. Debbie, miraculously, still off. Felt sure she'd have rushed back to work by now – she must be feeling rotten. Called at cottage but she was asleep. Didn't disturb her. Replenished supplies.

Phil's 75th. Took card and present down to Glebe, they are having all the family over tonight. Thought back to meeting Phil at start of year, trying to have polite conversation, but how I could hardly get my words out. Feel have come a long way. Even last little dip – Easter – more bearable. Feel the lows don't come as frequently or last as long, now, nor do I sink so far.

Thursday 24th April

4 p.m. Took Brian cup of tea and found him doing payroll. He casually mentioned he'd decided to pay Adam a wage, says he simply couldn't have managed without him with Debbie off. Adam, I know, was perfectly happy with bed and board – he's never been money-driven – main thing is, it's a big vote of confidence from Brian. Slight pang over Debbie – feel we are all leaving her out. But it's hard not to concentrate, like Brian did with Alice a month back, on those people from whom you're likely to get a positive response. Anyway, going to see her now, taking 'Echo' with picture of Lynda in undies. Look like Janet Reger, actually rather nice, though she has no bust and what the French delicately call 'heavy legs'.

6 p.m. No reply when I went down to cottage, let self in, no sign of Debbie. Momentary worry, then saw wellies and Barbour gone, must have gone for a walk. Left note, fruit, biscuits on table. She rang a few minutes ago – had been round fishing lake. Says she'll be back at work next week. Didn't sound very keen though. So unlike her not to be rushing back. Should be pleased she's taking all the rest she needs but not sure it's a good sign. Asked her to come to supper, she refused.

Monday 28th April

Adam cross with self, feels put foot in it with Debbie on first day back by mentioning the mildew he had to spray before Easter – the mildew she'd missed. She was immediately flagellating self, Adam tried to point out was eminently forgivable and anyway she was ill, Debbie not having any of it. On top of this he had to tell her about the strawberry idea, she said it sounded like a lot of work for very little. Have absolutely had enough of this. Am going to have a word with her.

Wednesday 30th April

Found moment to have word with Debbie, tried to claim she had to go and check on deer ready to calve but wasn't letting her get away that easily – even I know they are about the most trouble-free calvers in the animal kingdom. Asked how she was finding being back, she should make sure and ease self in gently, etc., she said she wasn't sure anyone had even noticed, they seemed to have managed perfectly well without her. Couldn't even find it in me to tell her this was nonsense, as actually has more than grain of truth – anyway she went straight on to say she wasn't surprised, she hasn't been pulling her weight lately, citing her total lack of interest in Hassett Hills, which I know has been bothering David. Then said she'd been doing a lot of thinking while she'd been off. She knew we were all sick of her being miserable, and she was sick of it herself – sick of seeing the same miserable face in the mirror every morning was how she put it. Poor sweetheart. Made me feel awful. Again said I/we'd do anything we could – if she'd just tell us how we could help her. She said we can't, she's got to do it for herself. And she's going to do something about it. Hallelujah!

DEPARTURE

Thursday 1st May

Have to say, can't see any immediate improvement in Debbie's temper or demeanour but know myself that it's one thing to make these resolves, another to carry them out.

She certainly didn't seem exactly gladdened by Adam saying at lunch that Brian has definitely OK'd his venison idea. The plan now is for us to convert a couple of outbuildings into a cutting room and cold room, get hold of a chiller cabinet for selling on the day, and ask George if he'd like to take a Marksman's Certificate so he can shoot them in the field. Adam did try and involve Debbie, asking her about butchers (luckily the idea is not for me to butcher them on kitchen table, as before!) but she wasn't exactly forthcoming. Adam suggested I knock out a leaflet about how we rear the deer – showed me some examples from his recces – and I thought we could also do one with recipes (would imagine a lot of people, though they might have eaten it out, might not have cooked venison at home). Brian delighted with this. Gave me a kiss, but very bad idea in front of Debbie, who promptly grabbed 'Farmers Weekly' and 'Sugar Beet Review', said she was going back to cottage for a bit.

Parish Council elections. Voted for David, of course. Graham Ryder's platform seems to be dog mess/anti-Grundies, which will no doubt garner him plenty of votes from Glebelands.

Friday 2nd May

David elected with sizeable majority. Spent all day doing large feature on website and fending off Lynda, who is determined to make a thing about Joe Grundy's pole barn. Worked in garden for Open Gardens at end of month: talk of gardening correspondent of Echo/Radio Borsetshire judging it. Mum and Jack very keen, Jack pulling out all stops in greenhouse. Says he'll bring on a few cuttings for me.

I'm happy to leave all the spinning to Lynda Snell and her llamas these days, but I was quite into it myself when I had the Jacobs, a present from Brian when we were first married.

Sunday 4th May

Alice a bit disappointed Debbie didn't come as promised to see her ride in Pony Club jumping competition, claiming she had 'lots of reading' to catch up on. Alice did very well in her class, qualified for final round against the clock, then came in third! Shula only slightly less ecstatic than Alice, think she's living out through Alice some of her own unfulfilled ambitions in the show ring. Also told me a bit about the new vicar we're getting in August. Alan Franks – widower, apparently, though only in forties, with daughter, Amy, about Alice's age. Alice says firmly I am not to try and throw them together, there are important questions to be answered first. Will or Gareth? (Hopefully neither.) Ms Dynamite or Mis-teeq? (Both.) And most importantly – does she like horses?

wednesday 7th May

Brian stomping round in filthy mood as Declan, the agronomist, here and Debbie had absented herself. Says if this is her 'new start', come back sullen features and silence. Took it out on Greg, who's finally reappeared from extended trip to France, claiming problems with his elder girl. Brian told him he wasn't interested, we all had family worries, etc., Greg seemingly chastened. Am with Pat in thinking he's not right for Helen – such a misery!

Debbie finally back end of the afternoon, didn't say where she'd been but looked very smart, wearing trouser suit I made her buy in Underwoods' sale last year. First wondered if she'd finally taken herself off for counselling of some sort, but can't really believe it. Am now wondering if perhaps she'd had a date, though when said this to Brian he practically fell on floor in amazement. With whom?? I pointed out she'd spent all weekend closeted away 'reading', Brian countered they didn't as far as he knew have a Lonely Hearts column in 'Sugar Beet Review', maybe he should suggest it. But they're in every paper these days, and what's to stop her? Would be very sensible way to put toe back in pool. Whatever reason for absence, hopefully a good sign. Part of this 'doing something' resolve.

Friday 9th May

Another good sign: Debbie took morning off (this time having warned Brian) to go to launch of 'Jaxx Caff' – formerly Daphne's. Mum said she seemed on good form, talking to Ruth and Usha mostly, and that Kenton was pleased she'd made the effort. Mum still a bit tight-lipped about wisdom of Jack's investment, both money in café and faith in Kenton, but he is on a six-month trial contract, so there's a get-out if needed.

Adam out again to Felpersham with these friends from the gym, sound a lively crowd. Asked Debbie to go too, but she said she'd got stuff to do, tidying cottage, chucking stuff out. Sounds as though she's doing a bit of a 'life laundry' – can only be a good thing. Would have been her wedding anniversary next Monday – perhaps this has prompted it.

Tuesday 13th May

Horrid moment in shop when Jill, chatting, revealed Elizabeth and Nigel are off to Ireland at the end of the week for Ruairi's christening. Had to cluck and smile, Betty immediately launched into 'Ooh, Siobhan, how is she?' routine – fine, apparently, not that I wanted to know. Wonder if Brian knows about it.

Friday 16th May

This afternoon found Brian sitting on bed delving in old suitcase, surrounded by his A-level certificates, school shooting trophies and ticket stub from Cilla Black concert! Sheepishly said he must have been affected by Debbie's de-cluttering and he couldn't think why he'd kept all this junk. I think he should hang onto it, there were things relating to his family, too, photos of his parents and so on, stuff belonging to his grandfather... am sure he'd regret it if he chucked it out.

Debbie at least civil, came in for cup of tea, chatted with Brian about harvest, Hassett Hills. A long way off 'normal' but better than has been. Said matter-of-factly that she got her decree absolute this week – on her anniversary, of all days. But maybe she feels the line's finally been drawn: sometimes you need something from outside yourself to do it. But please let this be start of a thaw for her and Brian.

Sunday 18th May

Adam hasn't hung about with his strawberry idea – wisely, before Brian could change his mind, he took himself off last week to visit a fruit co-op, joined it, came back, promptly deep ploughed the field and this week is getting a grower to come over to help construct the beds! So this morning he was out at seven with the tractor and cultivator working the land down, then off to cricket all day. Reportedly Sid very pro Adam, keeps hinting he'd make a better captain than Alistair, Adam spends as much time tactfully deflecting that as opposition balls. Round to Mum's, she's still fuming about Jack stupidly getting Higgs to lop a tree last week, with result that branch crashed down through her greenhouse, smashing a load of bedding plants. Can't see where she'd have put them anyway, beds are like a public park as it is, regimental salvias, aquilegia, marigolds. All she needs now is a floral clock.

Wednesday 21st May

Strawberry man today with special machine to earth up the strawberry beds – now all that remains is small matter of putting in the plants – all 25,000 of them! Not quite as bad as it sounds, Adam says, as they'll only (!) be putting in 5,000 a week, to stagger the cropping. Tried to entice Alice and me into helping – I said fine if he's going to pick up bill for osteopath, am already aching from weeding for Open Gardens. Alice said

147

she might at half term if she was bored.

Thursday 22nd May

Wedding anniversary next week. Not sure what to do. Brian hasn't said anything. Are we ignoring it, like Valentine's Day?? Is he waiting for me to suggest something? Or doesn't he think we have much to celebrate?

Friday 23rd May

Chris says you can't get a moment's peace round the green for the sound of lawnmowers, hedge trimmers and secateurs as people put on last spurt for Open Gardens – in between showers, as weather has really turned this week, just in time for silage making of course. Excitement now fever pitch as has been revealed celebrity judge is not Ted Hargreaves of 'Echo' but, in last-minute scoop, Alan Titchmarsh, apparently acquaintance of Jean Harvey's cousin! Had no idea the Harveys or indeed their rellies moved in such exalted circles, though as Alan T. famously down-to-earth, perhaps not that exalted. Betty, Clarrie, etc., devotees of his novels, all in complete tizz, Lynda trying to jump on bandwagon by offering to have her llamas pull him round village in a cart like some three-ring circus. Betty with remarkable sang froid informed her (deliciously, I was there) that she'd already arranged for Joe and Bart to do the honours. Lynda's face a picture. Offered to have him here for lunch, otherwise poor thing'll probably end up at Willow Farm for egg and chips, brown sauce optional. Betty said she'd come back to me.

7 p.m. Just had call from Betty. She's taking Alan to The Bull for lunch. And had already ordered the salmon!

Adam and Debbie to cinema to see *Matrix Reloaded* – is it my imagination or is she really a bit more cheerful?

Weather still very mixed and forecasters hedging their bets for the weekend. Fingers crossed for Monday, anyway, when Alan T. will be here.

Sunday 25th May

Couldn't wait for proper look round gardens, went as soon as they opened, also Adam and Debbie. Lynda hectoring everyone to keep to the paths, worried her grass would get churned up, Joe Grundy maundering on about how unfair it was she'd had a professional designer in. Don't see what he had to grouse about as he has basically copied all her ideas – water feature (one-armed statue on barrel with hose pipe in rear like enema), garden lighting (fairy lights left over from Grundy World of Christmas)... the list goes on. Clarrie had beautiful pot of lilies, though. Mum's garden immaculate, Glebe charming, and Chris and George have done wonders at The Police House. Didn't go around Derek Fletcher's, front is all pampas grass and block paving, and believe back is chiefly gnome-fringed fishpond!

Monday 26th May

Alan T. absolutely charming – got him to sign one of his gardening books which Phil and Jill gave me one Christmas – might even read one of his novels now. Didn't get a prize for garden (didn't really expect to) but Mum thrilled at coming second and Chris and George were, everyone agreed, worthy winners. Even weather bucked up.

wednesday 28th May

Spent all afternoon on website – like the garden, little and often is the answer – quite a few e-mails had come in about the Open Gardens so put together a feature showing Alan in Joe's trap, a list of winners and about a hundred words giving taster of the whole day. Thought worked rather well.

Had just decided we must be ignoring our anniversary when Brian suggested we go to Botticelli's. Says 27 years is worth celebrating – and that he wants us to celebrate many more. Felt quite teary.

Thursday 29th May

Very tactful card from Brian – just one of those black and white film stills, no gush, nothing over-the-top, think he's learned his lesson. Also fabulous lilies again but no little black leather box – thank goodness. Have had enough guilt presents to last me a lifetime. Got out the ring he bought me last year – wondered why I deserved a diamond – also the eternity ring he bought me at Christmas. It's absolutely beautiful – but I can't wear it. Tried the diamond on, though. Think I'll wear it tonight.

Into Felpersham to have hair done, also had manicure – well, if am drawing attention to hands with ring... all that gardening, despite gloves, has done nails no good at all. Brian out when I got back, Debbie looking for him. Said try proposed venison cold room or strawberry beds, also suggested she and Alice got video and had girls' night in while we were out tonight. Perhaps on reflection neither comment very tactful, only underlined Adam and Brian's joint commitment to new enterprises whilst casting her and Alice as sad Cinderellas. Anyway she gave me sort of sneery look, commented on hair and nails, said she was glad I was 'getting something out of it' and that I thought it was 'worth the effort'. Decided to seize the moment, so told her she had to stop making life impossible for herself, torturing herself over the fact that I'd decided to take Brian back, even though she didn't agree with it. Of course she managed to turn it round, saying that what I meant was that she was making life impossible for the rest of us (well she has been, nearly) – and when I tried to say that I simply didn't want her tearing herself to pieces over it, retorted that what she thought obviously didn't matter to me any more. Of course tried to say it did, not sure she believed me, but did firmly say that what went on between Brian and me was between Brian and me and she just had to let us get on with it. Don't feel good about saying it so bluntly, but it had to be said. Should in fact have said it long ago, leaving this long has only made things worse.

12 a.m. Lovely, lovely evening. Brian and I really seem to know where we're going now – those parallel tracks at the beginning of the year have definitely merged together again.

We really, properly, talked – felt really close to him. Talked about the children - Brian getting on so well with Adam, says he couldn't have coped with how Debbie's been towards him without Adam around, which is lovely to hear. Then about Debbie: seems a bit better, but neither of us can see a real way forward for her – both still so worried about her. And then, because we were getting on so well, I even felt safe to bring up Roger – well, by implication – and my affair with him. Because – and it's an extraordinary word to use about someone who has by most standards behaved appallingly – what I've admired about Brian in the last few months – something I've always admired – has been his strength of character. His integrity, his dignity in dealing with this, with me. When I think of all the recriminations I threw at him (not to mention the perfume) – how I dragged up his past misdemeanours – real, imagined, Caroline, Mandy – and yet he never, never once, mentioned Roger. When I put it to him tonight, he said I had much more to forgive than he ever had, but I don't know – I'm not sure that the fact that Roger was my ex-husband doesn't make it somehow worse. Suppose the bad side is that Brian's ego is so massive it wasn't dented by it, but still think it must have been a huge blow to his pride. Anyway, we had a sort of rueful chuckle (not meant to sound blasé) – he said what had we put ourselves through? – but in the end what we've put ourselves through is a marriage, with all its ups and downs. And if the fact that we're still together after 27 years is a miracle – well, it's still something to celebrate.

Anyway, the warmth between us just seemed to grow and grow and when we got back – I suppose we'd both had a bit to drink, we were both pretty relaxed – I went to put the kettle on for coffee and he was standing right next to me and I half turned and looked at him and he made this sort of half move towards me and the next thing I knew we were kissing, and not tentatively, but both really wanting each other. Came upstairs and made love for the first time in over six months. Wonderful.

Friday 30th May

8 a.m. Ridiculous. Feel like a teenager. Woke up with absurd smile on my face and Brian, when he brought me a cup of tea just now, exactly the same. So happy. I love him, he loves me.

6 p.m. Oh, my god. Exactly a month since Debbie said she'd got to pull herself together and do something to sort herself out and though it hasn't seemed like it to us, she obviously has been – has gone and got herself a job! In France! Can't take it in, am sure this is not the right option, at least not so precipitately, but she seems convinced, is talking about leaving on Monday, and has rushed off to pack as they want her as soon as possible!

Has been very topsy-turvy day all round. Wonderful dream-like morning, then kitchen this afternoon like a French farce. Alice had been whining on about wanting Debbie to go for a ride, but as Brian had just persuaded her into the office to look through some figures – Debbie had for once shown a spark of interest – sent Alice out to strawberry field to help Adam and Mike. Ten minutes later, Alice back, (strawberry planting 'too boring'), Brian and Debbie still closeted, so had to deflect her (teenagers so like toddlers) into making flapjacks. Just hunting for sultanas (trust Alice to complicate things) when Debbie stormed through, followed by Brian. Alice, fearing for loss ride, shouts at Brian, flings down wooden spoon, leaves syrup boiling on Aga, and flounces out after Debbie into yard. I'm left mopping up trails of goo, Brian looking haunted.

Seems – not quite sure how I can be so calm about this, but ironically, just as Debbie's problems at end of last year were subsumed by Brian and Siobhan, now Siobhan's been subsumed by Debbie – which is as it should be! In fact, I do know how I can be so calm about it, it was the way Brian told me. Simple, calm, matter-of-fact. I just don't feel – especially after the night we had last night – that there's the emotion there between him and her any more. Him and the baby, yes, that's different, that I can understand.

153

Anyway, completely out of the blue, without any instigation, she'd suddenly e-mailed him some photos – of Ruairi's christening. Brian had printed them off and – I don't know, I can't know what goes through his mind – I suppose he'd kept them in his desk drawer, looked at them a few times and then – yesterday he'd thrown them away. Which is terrible, really. His son – it breaks your heart. Except that it was our anniversary and, as he kept saying last night, over and over again, he loves me – me – and he's made his choice. The point is, not thinking, he let Debbie look through the bin for some papers he'd mislaid and she found the wretched things. Accused him of still being in touch with Siobhan, of lying again and again, of having me, Adam, Alice fooled – all the same old stuff, really.

Except this time it's different. First, because I'm with Brian on this, I believe him when he says he's not in contact, he didn't ask for the pictures. Siobhan's consigned, if not to the past, then at least into some kind of limbo, where she'll always remain, because of Ruairi, and I have to accept that. But he's chosen: he's with me, and I want to be with him. And secondly, though we didn't know it at the time, because Debbie had a way out.

Am going down to see her after supper. Can of course see why she's tempted – new start, away from it all – plus it's the most terrible blow she could possibly deal to Brian – but does it have to be France? And so soon? Will it help her sort herself out or is she just running away? If only she'd discussed it with someone.

154

Sunday 1st June

Have spent all weekend trying to talk to Debbie about this job –
Business Development Manager for a seed company based in Rheims –
they especially want someone bilingual as there are so many British
farmers over there and someone who's actually English will, they feel,
give them the edge. She seems absolutely sold on it, and I can see it
sounds very interesting – all I was trying to get her to do was to put
them off for a week so she doesn't have to leave in such a hurry,
especially after Friday, when she was so churned up again. She says
Friday had nothing to do with it, she'd had the offer and was going to
accept the job anyway, but I'm not so sure.

Brian absolutely devastated. Debbie says he's only worried about the
spray programme and the harvest, and there's no need, it's all on the
computer. Brian adamant he's to blame, it's all his fault Debbie's cut
herself off, though told him that's not true, she actually feels excluded
because of the two of us, me and him – she even said something today
about how we'd doubtless prefer it without her around to spoil the
'romantic atmosphere'. It's bizarre, really, it's as if she's the one who's
taken on the role of the wronged wife - except with the wrong husband.

Meanwhile Adam, who knew, apparently, that she'd gone for the
interview, is castigating himself for not trying harder to stop her. Like
me, he can see why the idea of getting away appeals, but he's not
convinced she had to take the first job she was offered – with her skills,
he's sure she could find a job in this country. Alice has gone horribly
quiet – out all yesterday and most of today on Spearmint. Clearly very
upset. She's really going to miss her.

Jennifer's Diary

Monday 2nd June

11 a.m. Filling time, really, till Debbie leaves at lunchtime. She's resolute about going: has told them she'll be there by Wednesday for a few days' training, then proper starting date June 9th. Spoke to this M. Hubert she's been dealing with when he rang for her: they've fixed her a company flat, which at least means she's not in some dingy hotel. At least it seems properly organised.

Alice off school today with transparent headache and Brian awake all night, tormenting himself about things. He went over to the cottage earlier to try to... well, he said he didn't quite know. Apologise? (Again?) Get her to change her mind? (Some chance). Debbie of course replied he only cared because of the farm, whereas she had a clear conscience, she wasn't leaving him in the lurch thanks to Adam (that's the other thing, he's now blaming himself because he feels he pushed her out, cuckoo in the nest, etc.). Brian told Debbie that Adam (in nicest sense) is no replacement, he's got livestock experience, yes, but nothing like hers on the arable, or in lots of other areas. Debbie predictably unmoved.

Can't think what I'm going to do for the next two hours. Suppose could make her some sandwiches for train, know they have souped up Eurostar but mainly for first class as far as I can gather. Yes, sandwiches. And some proper English tea bags to take with her.

2 p.m. Debbie gone: Adam took her to train, was sure she wouldn't want me weeping all over her on the platform. Had trouble stopping Alice from going with them – car had hardly left yard before she was sending Debbie a text – but Debbie has cleverly given her Tolly to look after, so was able to suggest she went straight and gave him good curry

156

combing. Big hugs all round except for Brian, of course – awful pause when he mumbled something about thinking the world of her – daren't say how much he loves her. She did manage to say something in reply, thank goodness, even if purely for Alice's sake, then just got in car.

Brian and I left standing there, a real couple of lost souls. He very sensibly suggested we went in and had a glass of wine, which, if not a solution, was certainly a palliative. Funny, a few months ago I'd have been the first one to blame him for Debbie going, but that was when we were living in parallel, and everything else was bent out of shape and distorted. Now, if anything, Debbie seems to be blaming both of us. She must be very unhappy indeed if she can't bear anyone else to be happy.

The truth is, I'm terrified for her – not just about France, about settling in, about the suddenness and the strangeness of it all – I'm worried about her full stop. She was so damaged by what happened last year, and in the last few months she's damaged herself, and sometimes when people are damaged they just don't care any more. At least with her here, I could keep some sort of check on her. Now she's really on her own – no support. But from her point of view, I suppose, no reminders of what's been dragging her down, either.

DISCLOSURE

Tuesday 3rd June

Phone call from Debbie, just to say she'd arrived safely, flat very nice with view over typical little French square, café, pâtisserie, pharmacy, etc. First day in new job tomorrow. They are also giving her a car. Very strange without her, Alice quite lost, after school following Adam around as if she's scared to let him out of her sight. Very bad timing for her, with end of year exams next week.

Wednesday 4th June

David round this evening, obviously worried about the implications of Debbie not being here both for Hassett Hills and the Brookfield harvest. Brian twitchy as a result. Said I'd do what I could to help, which I realise will be mostly (wo)manning stall at farmers markets – can rope Alice in once holidays start, plus she can collect riding course fees whilst I do fishing lake.

Adam has got to learn combine and get Certificate of Competence for spraying: Brian says we may have to bite the bullet and fork out for Declan (agronomist) to come in a bit more often, but apart from that, we'll be fine. Hope David sees it like that.

Debbie and Alice texting/phoning like mad – Alice about Tolly, Debbie about job. All in firm seem very nice people. She says the difference between here and England is the men have handbags and the women have briefcases! Also that the coffee and hot chocolate is to die for but she's glad of her teabags. Reassuring to know am still a good mother in some respects.

Friday 6th June

Aching all over, having helped Brian select lambs for abattoir – had forgotten how mulish sheep can be. Adam plastering deer larder, held up by Sid wittering on again about him becoming cricket captain. Wish he would leave Adam alone, he's got enough to think about at the moment. So have I, without Lynda Snell nagging me about setting up a message board alongside the website. According to her, there wasn't enough 'local colour' in my report on the Open Gardens, and seems to think a public forum for every crank and attention-seeker in the village is the answer. If she could see some of the e-mails I get from Derek Fletcher she wouldn't be quite so keen, but as she's prepared to set it up and moderate it, couldn't really be bothered to argue, it'll get him off my back anyway.

Debbie rang again: have spoken more to her in the last few days than I have for months – not that I'm complaining. M. Hubert (and wife) have invited her to supper tonight, which is sweet: at least she won't be on her own, though as she says, in France it's perfectly possible for a woman to have a meal or a drink in a café without attracting either pitying stares or lecherous attention. Adam and Alice spoke to her as well, though when Alice mentioned it at supper Brian went very quiet, obviously hurt we hadn't called him to have a word. Had to say we weren't sure where he was, though know he was in the office. Very awkward. He said next time to be sure to tell Debbie he was missing her and to send his love. Ached all over again, for both of them.

Sunday 8th June

Single Wicket – very exciting final, Adam v. Alistair, but Alistair bowled Adam l.b.w. so Shula ended up presenting the trophy to her own husband. Must have been hard for her, actually, noticed Phil having a quiet word afterwards. Sid also took Adam on one side, questioning Phil's impartiality as umpire – more a case of Sid's partiality to Adam, I think. Good to see Adam relaxing properly for once, he and Brian were at it all day yesterday, finishing off the deer larder floor. The meat hygiene man is coming this week, George has got his Marksman's Certificate, so Adam hopeful we'll ready for our first farmer's market by the end of the month!

Monday 9th June

Inevitable, I suppose, but Brian's working far too hard covering for Debbie – and certainly not just displacement activity re: missing her. Looked quite grey with tiredness when he (finally) came in tonight, annoyed with self because Eddie Grundy had had to remind him about coming over to make small bales. Quite ridiculous – when's he had time to think? Told him he'll drive himself into the ground by harvest if he's not careful. Still, at least with all this on his plate he can't have a second to be thinking about Siobhan and Ruairi in a 'this-time-last-year' kind of way. Strange how life seems to stay the same for ages, then suddenly moves you on headlong whether you like it or not.

wednesday 11th June

Mum wanted me for a fête committee meeting but Brian needed me here to take in a couple of deliveries and point a rep. in direction of where he was spraying. Had enough last year, anyway, suggesting that football match – which turned into a lot of work devising rules.

Have to say website load has eased – inbox blissfully free of bonkers e-mails now we've set up link from website to Lynda's message board. It rejoices in the name of 'Ambridge Chat' (or 'Ambridge Pointless Wittering' as Brian calls it). Moderating is absolutely made for Lynda (or the other way round) – she loves leaping in with 'this correspondence is now closed' (subject was 'Another bench on the green?') and slapping people down when they get too frivolous. And, to her credit, she has let through a couple of anti-llama postings – as she keeps telling me, her role is to moderate, not to censor. Brian says if he had more hours in the day he would send an anti-Lynda message and see if that got posted. Reminded him that am sure libel laws apply even in cyberspace.

Thursday June 12th

Adam off on theory module for spraying course today, but at least he's taking the evening off for Nigel's birthday drinks at Lower Loxley. He says Elizabeth's upset Debbie left for France without a word – I can't see why, she must know Debbie felt as betrayed by Elizabeth as anyone. Brian still working as if demented, he's got to stop – this is supposed to be a relatively quiet time! Delegating, though, not his strong point – have explained to Adam it took Debbie years to carve out her areas of responsibility – but if he'd only take ten minutes to talk Adam through a few things, Adam'd be able to be much more help, even though he can't take on burden of spraying just yet. Adam and Mike still strawberry planting, too: Adam feeling guilty having suggested all these new enterprises which we now need like a hole in the head. I disagree: it's exactly the things Adam's initiated which have given Brian back his interest in the farm.

Alice keeping Tolly to show standards with daily grooming, plus lots of time out on Spearmint and at Stables in prep. for Pony Club Show on 29th. Poor Chandler hardly gets a look-in, though she did give Phoebe a little ride on him today after school. You could see the poor creature thought it was his birthday. Tried to ask Alice how her exams were going: 'They're exams, Mum'. No wiser.

Friday 13th June

Mum round fretting about fête committee meeting: though they've got all the usual things, they're lacking that extra something (the football match equivalent) which is what really pulls in the crowds. Lynda has suggested 'Guess the Weight of the Llama' but they don't feel this is enough. Hope Mum's not looking to me for inspiration – sponsored strawberry-plant perhaps? She also wants Alice to get the Pony Club to do a display – suppose she will at least have finished school by then. She went off this morning saying how was anyone expected to do well in an exam on Friday 13th? Brian says until they offer Horse and Pony Maintenance as an option, not much point Alice doing GCSEs next year anyway.

Wrote piece for website publicising the GM meeting which Jill's organising via the WI: such a relief to have only fact, not opinion, to concentrate on. Lynda is more than welcome to the message board. Most of Jolene's 'Leisure' page is pushing their Nettle Eating Competition on Midsummer's Day, have to say she is inventive. They should ask her on to fête committee.

Food hygiene chap has given thumbs up to 'Deer Larder: The Story So Far' but is coming back to see it when it's completely finished. Don't know what else he expects, gold-plated paper-towel holder perhaps, but Pat says this is normal, Tom went through same rigmarole with his sausage unit.

Brian beside himself at lunchtime as David over in filthy temper: had found huge patch of blight on Brookfield spuds. Brian blamed the weather – very iffy for spraying this week, windy, or if not wind, sudden showers – but David says Debbie would have found the right moment and blight would never have happened. Brian more cross with self than anything else – has promised to spray them personally at weekend. David says this is too late. Does not bode well for good relations at harvest.

However, one bright spot: Adam has offered to do routine maintenance on combine, sort of thing he was used to doing all the time in Africa, no calling out the engineer there. It'll save us up to £200 even though the chap'll still have to come out for the electrics, Adam won't touch those. Think Adam is keen to prove that, though of course he can't step into Debbie's management role straight off, there are other things he can offer which are time/cost saving. We'll have to have a student for harvest after all, though, just hope he/she won't have to stay in house. Agonised, but since she's sounding so settled in France already, put Debbie's cottage back with agency midweek and was promptly booked for all of August, so no chance of student staying there. Brian is going to ask around at Borsetshire Ag. College re: student, see if we can get someone local who could live at home.

Sunday 15th June

Not quite the Father's Day I'd planned – nor Brian, come to that – as he was up at five to do David's wretched spraying. Rewarded him with proper breakfast when he got back, Alice pleased he'd liked her card but clear he was on tenterhooks all day in case Debbie should 'phone. She didn't, but then she'd phoned yesterday. Tried to pacify Brian saying the Huberts had told her to use their pool anytime, she'd probably gone there today. Must be a novelty for her not having to work weekends. Her phone calls – apart from to Alice – are getting less frequent, which is, I suppose, a good sign, though her evident happiness in France is rather incontrovertible proof that it was the atmosphere here that was getting her down. Brian and I talked about this but, in the end, it was an atmosphere of her own making. Sounds awful to say it, but if anyone had time to stop and take note, the atmosphere here has probably eased too.

Glorious day, spent it by pool. Hillary Clinton interviewed in paper (has book out) talking about having to take a long hard look at her marriage, her husband and herself. Sounds familiar.

Monday 16th June

Mum dragged me to fête committee meeting at The Bull when should have been collecting fishing lake money but at least Jolene has come up with something as main attraction – wife carrying! She found it on the

Internet – some ancient tradition somewhere in world, apparently. Women in sort of fireman's lift, lugged round obstacle course by their loved one, prize is woman's weight in beer! Can see men going for it, but also problem straight away: what woman is going to let herself be weighed in public to claim prize? We bought the idea anyway.

Wednesday 18th June

Am definitely going to see about a new kitchen: feelings about it as backdrop to ongoing kitchen sink drama vindicated again today when was the setting for Adam telling me he is gay. Don't quite know what I think about this revelation. Suppose I should be shocked, but in all honesty, can't really say it came as huge surprise: more confirmed what I'd already sort of suspected. Let's face it, when your son's nearly thirty-six, fabulous-looking, clever, funny, capable, kind, etc., etc. and hasn't ever brought home a girl who wasn't 'just a friend', you do, just gently, start to wonder. And, as time goes on, and he hasn't been snapped up, or let himself be snapped up, by one of the predatory thirty-somethings with ticking wombs you're always reading about, you do tend to ask yourself why. You also, if you're me, even without the pitying enquiries of friends and family and the crass 'but don't you miss him?' comments, have to ask yourself why – apart, of course, from a fine-tuned sensibility and social conscience – why Adam would choose to take off to ever-more-remote parts of Africa throughout those very years when his contemporaries were settling down and getting steady jobs, then steady girlfriends, then steady mortgages. But at the same time – I suppose I hadn't entirely written off the possibility that he was just taking his time. And he is, after all, a very private person. While this Maggie who's been writing and phoning was a bit of a red herring.

Anyway, it turns out the person in Africa who broke his heart, the one he mentioned, was, in fact, a man – and it was a grand passion, on Adam's part at least. But this chap – Alex – he's half-French, some kind of travel rep. – was ready to move on sooner than Adam was – literally. He got himself some work in the Gambia, and poor Adam, not reading the signs – well, that was when Adam moved to Senegal, to be closer to him, but it was all over as far as Alex was concerned. Adam still didn't realise, tried to keep it going – got desperately hurt in the process. Hate to think of him going through all that alone. Sensibly went back to Kenya, though, to lick his wounds, and that's where he got so friendly with Maggie and who Mum was convinced was a girlfriend. More a sort of mother-confessor, by the sound of it.

So there it is. Adam's big secret, out in the open – well, to me, anyway.

Thursday 19th June

9 a.m. Have been thinking a lot about yesterday – think have felt almost numbed since Debbie left, almost couldn't take in Adam's news. Waking up to it doesn't change how I feel, but am starting to wonder/worry how everyone else will react.

Can't see Mum taking it very well – she's been asking pertinent questions about Adam's love life ever since he got back, you can see she's just itching to get him married off when frankly, after the disasters Debbie and I have had with our marriages, you'd think she'd be a bit more circumspect. It's her generation, I suppose, always yearning for a happy, orange-blossom-scented ending. And, to be fair, I suppose with advancing years, there's a tendency to want to see all the loose ends tied up. Well, Adam's one she won't be able to knot neatly into life's rich tapestry – not sure she'd feel the same about a 'marriage' ceremony with a boyfriend!

Not at all sure about Brian, either. Adam asked me how I thought he should proceed, but Brian's so exhausted and stressed, don't feel he should even broach it at the moment. It's not as though anything's going to be different – but you just never know how people will react, and Brian... well, I'm not sure. Also can't help wondering what Paddy would make of it?! He was such a – well, blokeish sort of man – the classic macho, red-blooded, Alpha male. He'd probably blame me and think it was because he wasn't around to take Adam to football matches and teach him to tear off bottle-tops with his teeth. I suppose in a way I am to blame. Doesn't all the research say that gay men have preternaturally close relationships with their mothers? And look at Adam's early life... me and him, one-to-one, then Mum, Lilian, me and him at The Bull. Dad and Tony weren't exactly around enough to be any kind of influence and even if they had been, it would hardly have been beneficial, Dad with his drinking and Tony obsessed with sports cars and chasing women. Then there was Roger, fair enough, but that didn't last, and pretty soon we were on our own again, me and Adam, with Debbie only a toddler. And then moving in with Chris, to keep her company when Paul was away so much. And the way Adam idolised Peter – another one with a few traumas in his life – adopted, then losing Paul altogether. Of course, he's not married, either.

What did we do to them, these boys? That's nonsense, we didn't do anything, just made the best of the pretty unsatisfactory situations their respective fathers – adoptive, natural, step – had left us in. Anyway so much for boys needing strong male role models – where were mine, let alone Adam's?

2 p.m. Tried to talk to Adam after lunch about what I'd been thinking, but he's not having any of it, laughed out loud, absolutely refuses to let me psychologise it, says it's genetic, and anyway, he's not looking for reasons, it's just how it is. And he's right, of course – when he's so sorted about things, it's almost insulting to try and look for explanations, my own form of not really accepting it, to try and make it fit some predetermined psychological pattern.

But it hasn't stopped me thinking about myself, and what I went through when Adam was a baby – before that, even, when I knew I was pregnant – all over again. When I look at the men in my life – what exactly was I looking for all those years? It's not as easy as saying 'a father substitute' – not that my father ever was much of a father. Arguably, given that Mum and Lilian and I ended up looking after him, I might just as well have been looking for someone else to watch over. I'm not even sure there's a pattern. I'm not sure there even was a seeking after something, subconscious or not.

Paddy and me – if that wasn't just chemistry, what was it? Biology? I certainly didn't plan to have a baby. But when I found out I was – well, I could have had Adam adopted. Enough people wanted me to. I could even (though illegally) have had an abortion. It was my decision not to. And what was I expecting from Mum and Dad, really? Did I want Dad to step in to protect me somehow, to tell me what to do? When he tried to play the Victorian father that certainly didn't seem right. And even if getting pregnant had been some deep-down desire to get him to notice me (which I don't honestly think it was) then to notice me as what? His little girl who needed looking after, or a grown up who was putting up two fingers and saying 'You've made me play the adult since I was a child, well, I've got a child of my own now, is that adult enough for you?'.

And then, with that all still a muddle, and Adam a baby, to be catapulted almost straight into Roger, when he was still involved with Lilian. But everyone being so grateful to him, and amazed he'd 'take me on', and me feeling the same, unable to believe my luck, when he could have gone for someone so much more straightforward. Except Roger had plenty of complications of his own, didn't he, with not getting on with his parents and changing his name and everything? Maybe marrying me was his own two-finger moment to that dreadful snooty mother of his. Maybe he liked coming over as the knight in shining armour. Or maybe what we recognised in each other was that we were both a bit screwed up.

It should have worked, Roger and me, it really should. He really was everything I wanted. He had the lot – well-off, cultured, good-looking – everything I admired. Intellectually, not just physically, we were so well matched. Still were when he turned up again all those years later – seeing him again, talking to him again was electrifying. Real conversations about things that mattered, things we shared. So powerfully, desperately sexy. God, though, I should never have slept with him again. If it had really had anything going for it surely we'd have stayed together all those years ago? But you kid yourself, don't you, that it was just the wrong place, the wrong time... Not that that's any excuse for the damage it did Debbie. The damage I did Debbie.

Which only leaves Brian. My second chance at happiness, everyone thought – another union heavily promoted by my ever-loving family, who must by then have been getting seriously worried. Gran to

Grandad, I can just imagine: 'Look at our Jennifer, two children and not a father between them. Now who's this fellow you say's buying the Estate?' But how often do two fairytale princes ride into your life in quick succession? Or at all? I was supposed to be the clever one of the family, you'd have thought I'd have seen through all that nonsense. Was I really so ground down by then, so demoralised that I'd apparently 'failed' two children, that I let them tell me Brian was 'the one'? Pathetic of me if I did. I don't think that's how it was, actually. I think I put up quite a fight. Brian was too arrogant, I can remember telling Mum, too sure of himself. It all felt a bit mechanical – inherited the money, bought the farm, what's missing, ah, yes, the little wife to shackle to the stove. But of course, Brian played it very cleverly. Played me along until I was interested, if only through sheer disbelief that he seemed so resistant to my charms. Didn't propose and didn't propose and didn't propose, all over that dreadful Christmas – then suddenly popping the question early in the New Year, when I was off my guard. And so the once-independent, trail-blazing Jennifer became the domesticated creature Brian thought he wanted – and the minute I did, of course, had Kate and actually relaxed into that sort of everyday tedium which you take as happiness – well, he was off, wasn't he? It hadn't been what he wanted at all. Or it wasn't enough to keep him interested any more. And I sensed things weren't the same, and had to find something to do, and got involved with the landscape survey project, and John Tregorran got that peculiar crush on me, which was sort of flattering, but spooky at the same time, and the next thing was, though of course I didn't know it, Brian was running around with Caroline – perfect, how mature, tit for tat. But we got over that, we got over Mandy Beesborough, and we've got round, if not over, all the other liaisons and silly little affairs over the years. And lately, I think we really are starting to get over Siobhan.

171

In the end, of course, Brian wasn't my white knight at all. I'm not saying he's all black prince either – God knows, I've made my mistakes. But we work well together, Brian and I. We complement each other, and deep down, maybe we're more similar than we like to admit. We're both pragmatists, when it comes to it, but romantic pragmatists. He's worked bloody hard these last few months to win me round, and though you could say 'so he should', he wouldn't have done any of it if he didn't believe in us. OK, he's not perfect. Neither am I. Isn't that a much better basis for a relationship than expecting someone to rescue you from – and then make up for – all the bits of yourself and your situation that you don't like?

Friday 20th June

Not really any brain space to think about ordinary things for the last couple of days, but forced to earlier when encountered very subdued (for her) Lynda Snell. As predicted, she's fast seeing that the message board is a poisoned chalice. Seems someone calling themselves 'Foursquare' started a seemingly innocuous debate about parking round the green which she now realises had racist undertones. (That particular night was Usha's birthday bash at the village hall, lots of her family and friends there.) Lynda so dispirited, felt almost sorry for her. Brian on other hand says he can't believe someone has finally found a way of slowing her down, would like to shake 'Foursquare' by the hand.

4 p.m. Quizzed Adam again; admitted I was a bit hurt, deep down that he hadn't said anything to me before about being gay – since we're supposedly so close – and we had another long talk. He's quite clear he's not gay because of anything I did or didn't do – not my being a single mum, not my marrying Roger, or divorcing Roger, not my marrying

Brian and especially not sending Adam away to school. Which is nice to hear, as I've spent the last few days running the past through my head like old ciné film, wondering where I could possibly have gone right. Adam, so sensible, says I've got to stop looking for a reason and (reading my mind) above all blaming myself. He says straight people have difficult childhoods too and gave me an 'oh, please' look (so like Alice) when I said he'd always been special. Says that's almost as bad as 'different' – or, even worse, 'sensitive'! So we had a laugh about it, though what I meant really was special to me, because of what we went through together, just the two of us.

Suppose I should be flattered he's told me at all – with attitudes in Africa not that enlightened, he's got rather used to keeping it a secret. Oh, and for the record, he loved Sherborne – played all the sport he wanted and had a crush on his best friend!

6.30 p.m. Just when you thought it was safe to go back, etc., etc... Mum knows. That is, Adam's just told her – in the kitchen, of course, where else?!

Started out as one of those innocuous conversations about other people – Debbie, mainly. Turned into diatribe against Simon, perils of working too hard, Adam not to let Brian take advantage, how if he didn't carve out some time for himself, Adam would never meet a nice girl... So I'm cringing and trying to slide under the table, Adam to his credit is stifling a grin, when suddenly she comes out with the fact that Jack plays golf with some farmer near Worcester who's got a daughter evidently in the marriage market – the next thing is she's suggesting a cosy little dinner party – her, Jack, Adam and this girl! Frantic throwing on of wet blankets from me, tact from Adam, but she was so persistent that, thank God, Adam took charge and very sweetly but assertively said thanks but no thanks, truth is, he's gay. Deathly silence. Thankfully I had to fetch Alice from Stables, so beat hasty if cowardly retreat.

When we got back, Mum had gone – surprised she was in fit state to drive. Adam rather downcast, really felt her disapproval. It would have to come out now. We've got them coming round on Sunday for his birthday, which is clearly going to be agonising re-run of 'Abigail's Party' without even escape of alcohol. Can only hope Jack will take more of a 'live and let live' approach and calm Mum down a bit.

Saturday 21st June

Tried to ring Mum this morning, Jack said she was lying down with a headache. However they are still coming to tea tomorrow. So he doesn't put his foot in it, warned Jack that Brian doesn't know – Adam's decided to leave telling him for time being till we've dealt with the Mum problem. Am just going to do sponge with strawberries (not ours, yet, sadly) and mascarpone for cake – they may not stay long enough to have any.

Alice berating herself for poor performance at her riding lesson yesterday, says she may as well withdraw from next week's competition. Told her Debbie would be disgusted with her if she quit now, seemed to do the trick

Sunday 22nd June

7 p.m. Excruciating tea for Adam's birthday, even Brian noticed something was up. Luckily he had to leave halfway through to sort out some altercation at the fishing lake, or he'd probably have asked Mum

straight out what was going on, assuming she'd gone all huffy on him again. By end of afternoon felt like bit of chewed string, having to placate him, plus deal with Mum and poor embarrassed Jack. Not sure what was worst bit – Mum's gift of Tattersall checked shirt, the sort of thing David wears for best, or Jack somehow cornering Adam into describing some fearfully macho Kenyan initiation rite. Mum just didn't seem to know what to say, as if overnight Adam has morphed into some kind of monster. Adam putting on brave face but clearly hurt, though says she'll just have to tough it out, there's not much he can do. He's gone out with friends this evening, hope he can salvage something from the day.

Adam – home at last.

9 p.m. Just rang Mum to try to talk to her, had very stilted conversation, seems she's taking Adam's sexual orientation as personal slight. Says she's 'so worried' about him – seems to be non-specific worry: AIDS/HIV, of course, but also his never being able to have proper 'family life' (hah! Like at Home Farm, I suppose!). To be fair, the same things have flitted through my mind, but she is, I suppose understandably for her generation, more inclined to dwell on them. Some of the things she says are absolute howlers: 'But Jennifer, he was in the rugby team!' Meanwhile, Jack, bless him, thinks it's a case of Adam simply not having met the right girl yet! Bit tongue and pleaded with Mum to try to be understanding and not to judge, for Adam's sake.

Jennifer's Diary

Monday 23rd June

Sudden visit from Mum this morning, apologising for yesterday – and then immediately making things worse. Her idea of being 'understanding' was to surf the net for some 'So Your Child's Gay?' websites – she cannot get it into her head that I don't need a helpline, the only support we need is hers! Just the same when I told her I was pregnant – even when trying to be supportive, always this dreadful disappointed/disapproving look in her eyes. Also, marriage to Jack seems to have wiped her memory bank – seems to think marriage is answer to everything, as if by its nature happy – obviously forgotten long years of torture while Dad drank himself to death, or indeed what I've just been through. Quite ridiculous and told her so. Also, firmly, to love Adam for what he is, not what she wants him to be. She departed slightly chastened. I hope.

Wednesday 25th June

Adam says he almost thought of telling Brian this morning when they were out early with the deer but says wasn't quite the right moment. Think this thing with Mum has made him nervous.

Founder's Day at school so Alice on half day, immediately disappeared off to stables. Discovered why when found the exam results she'd extracted from post and hidden behind fruit bowl on dresser. As in Sciences and Geography but B in History and C in French – not terrible by any means, but nothing like her usual standard. Am not surprised after all the upheavals here, but Brian more inclined to blame the time she's been spending on horses – now three to look after including Tolly. When Alice finally appeared, he put it to her that Tolly should go into livery and/or we get rid of Chandler – outcry from Alice, Adam chipped in and said no point paying for livery as he was riding Tolly and could help with grooming. I couldn't face row and suggested we see how things go over summer hols, reconsider in September. Surely everything will have settled down by then?

Friday 27th June

Home Farm however, an oasis of tranquillity compared with Brookfield, where they are frantically grooming a Hereford for the Royal, and Pat and Tony's, where Tom and Fallon are even more frantically getting ready to go to Glastonbury. Reminded Brian that we are lucky Alice is into horses rather than music scene, also that his presence required at Pony Club Show on Sunday. Despite the occasional spat, Alice idolises him.

Sunday 29th June

As ever, work got in the way – Brian late to see Alice ride as had to stay back to meet the student we've had to take on for harvest. Also Adam at cricket match but Debbie called to say good luck, which bucked Alice up. Tried to point out I'd be there to cheer her on, but I don't count, of course. She makes it worse for herself by being so competitive, she absolutely has to get a rosette or whole thing a complete waste of time, in her view. Brian says if only she'd have the same attitude towards her schoolwork – not entirely fair, think we are more to blame than she is for results this year. Thankfully Brian arrived in time to see her in the jump-off – she ended up with second place, Shula will be thrilled. Brian got it all on video, too.

Adam also on good form, took another century in the cricket v. Borchester Old Boys (says he's got something to prove!) though awkward moment when Brian commented on village girls lusting after him in his whites – Adam is going to have to say something soon. Mum seems to have gone quiet on the matter, still licking her wounds from our last encounter, I think. Realise I haven't actively thought about how Brian and I are doing for ages – is this a good sign? Is that how you know you're better, when it isn't the first thing you think about when you wake up in the morning? Feels good, anyway. Comfortable. Dare I say it – normal life?

REVERBERATIONS

Tuesday 1st July

Full scale slanging match has broken out on message board between Joe Grundy and Foursquare over Joe's pony and trap, Bartleby's droppings, etc. Site is now only monitored, not moderated (time and effort needed for moderation too much even for Lynda), these rantings have been carrying on unchecked for days. Asked Lynda today exactly who Foursquare is, but she went all coy and said she couldn't reveal anyone's identity as a matter of principle. Joe, meanwhile, says Foursquare should not be allowed to carry on posting unchallenged whilst hiding behind alias. This is exactly the sort of thing I knew would happen if we started a message board. So glad I am nothing to do with it.

Wednesday 2nd July

At supper had lengthy discussion about GM crops in advance of debate about them at village hall, which Adam reports turned into a bit of a free-for-all: Susan Carter vociferous in support – cheaper food – Pat,

179

Tom and Tony predictably still very anti.

Brian and Adam are both in favour, though of course they come at it from completely different angles. (Had thought Adam would be against, along 'genie-out-of-the-bottle' lines, but he can see the potential for disease-resistant crops for the Third World. Brian simply thinks it's progress – and profit, presumably – says the antis are just scaremongering). Anyway, resulted in a bit more male bonding for the pair of them.

Would feel much happier if Adam would just tell Brian about being gay, but with Mum still not exactly won round – have hardly seen her this past week – think Adam feels he wants to pick them off one at a time. Have offered to tell Brian myself, but Adam says no, he'd rather do it himself – he'll find the right moment.

Thursday 3rd July

George round to shoot the first two deer today, then tutor Adam in the fine art of skinning and gutting. Went out to watch. Despite syrupy Bambi myth, deer in fact so unfeeling they hardly stopped grazing as first one fell dead among them. Skinning and gutting neither as straightforward, nor clean, but George says Adam'll soon get the knack. Meat inspector passed the carcasses anyway, so Brian and Adam love-in continues: only Adam being due at nets prevented Brian from cracking open one of his best Chablis in celebration, start of great things to come on farm, etc., etc., not to mention hope that Adam might score a third century in cricket on Sunday, and much ribald joshing about Adam's adoring female fan-base in the village. Like something out of 'The Golden Bough': as if Brian's handing on (but happily) mantle of lady-killer/dragon-slayer. If only he knew.

Friday 4th July

Joe Grundy is now riding around with a placard bearing the legend: 'Foursquare come out and be a man' on one side of his trap and 'Four legs not four wheels' on the other. And they say there are no 'characters' in villages any more!

Rang Debbie: sounds very well, says Rheims is getting into festive mode for Bastille Day, asked if Alice would like to go over and stay in August sometime. You bet she would.

Sunday 6th July

Cricket v. Waterley Cross today. Brenda Tucker there on behalf of Radio Borsetshire to interview Adam, a.k.a. 'rising young star of village cricket', about his two centuries and prospects for a third – goes out sometime this week. Brian still droning on endlessly about my talented son, how dashing he looks in cricket whites, etc. – the way he's carrying on, you'd think he fancied Adam himself.

Tuesday 8th July

Brian over to Brookfield to walk their barley: weather permitting, will start combining there on Monday. David still giving him a hard time about hoping all will go smoothly without Debbie in charge, but Brian says he's on edge because they've got a TB case at Bank Farm, which shares a boundary with Brookfield. Foursquare saga continues: Joe has now challenged him (her?) to a 'High Noon' type showdown in the pub. Meanwhile Lynda claims to have 50 signatures on her petition against the Grundys' pole barn.

Adam's interview went out this afternoon. Had told Mum – wasn't

181

expecting much feedback, but she was on phone as soon as it was over (dreadful link into 'Flying Without Wings', glad to switch it off). Full of praise for Adam: how nice it was to hear an intelligent, well-spoken young man on the local radio instead of all the usual mindless babbling. Adam says it's pretty embarrassing having your grandmother as your number one fan, though of course Brian was quick to point out there were in fact plenty of young women vying for that position. If anyone is embarrassing, he is.

Stan (Tom's butcher) has cut up deer into steaks, packs of diced forequarter and made venison sausages. Now first market almost upon us, (Friday) cannot believe we are really going through with it. What if no one buys and we end up carting it all back home? Adam too busy pre-harvest to be nervous, lucky thing.

wednesday 9th July

Brian harping on again to Adam last night, apparently, about Brenda Tucker fancying him. (That girl, honestly, this family seems to hold a fascination for her). Anyway, Adam couldn't bear it any longer, so tried to tell Brian about being gay, saying Brenda was an attractive girl, he could see why Brian might think, etc., etc… but Brian somehow got hold of wrong end of stick and seemed to think Adam was suggesting that he (Brian) was interested in Brenda!! Much awkwardness and back-pedalling on both sides, but before Adam could put him right, Tom turned up and chance was gone. Adam says he'll find another time, though with our harvest starting tomorrow, all being well, and our first farmers' market on Friday, can't see when he'll have a minute.

Thursday 10th July

First day of harvest reasonably hitch-free: just as well, as wanted some time to think through logistics of farmers' market. Haven't even got the chill counter yet, Adam and Brian have got to collect it tonight – all they need after a hard day on the combine.

Pat rang and told me Tony was in pub at time of Joe and Foursquare's supposed showdown. At the appointed hour, who should some through the door but Susan Carter – clearly not the person in question! So Joe is claiming a moral victory – and, furthermore, maintains that, having chickened out of the challenge, he doesn't see how Foursquare will dare say another word against him and Bart.

Speculation rife in village as to who Foursquare actually is. Derek Fletcher's name has obviously come forward, as has Graham Ryder's, through from my memory of it Foursquare started pontificating before we extended the right of posting to people who only worked in the village. And a rash of really silly ideas: Higgs; Mr Pullen; Neville Booth; Charles Harvey; and 'that funny bloke from Glebelands who always wears his shirt buttoned up to the neck'.

Friday 11th July

Debbie rang incredibly early – of course they're an hour ahead, was already at her desk – to say good luck with our first market, really sweet of her and big concession to Adam. Market an absolute eye-opener, by 11 a.m. hardly any steaks left! Forequarter and sausages slower to shift, but may not be the same story at every market, will have to get to know our clientele. Some lovely people there, both stallholders and customers, all very willing to chat and we made over £800!

Got back to find Brian and the men well into the barley, Adam had to get straight on with hauling grain, but Brian did let him off a bit early this evening for nets. As I feared, now harvest has started, Adam not sure when he'll find any time, let alone a good time, to tell Brian. Can see he now wishes he'd got it out of the way early on, it's one of those things that the longer you leave it, the worse it gets. Wish I could tell him the anticipation is bound to be worse than the reality, but can't honestly say I know how Brian'll react. And the more Brian fixes Adam in his mind as some kind of Lothario, the worse it'll be. As it was, we both had to endure nod-and-wink stuff about going to the pub after nets and 'bet we know who'll be there, don't we, Jenny?' Torture. When Adam had gone, tried to hint that, unlike Tom, for example, Adam was not girl-crazy, but Brian has picked up the phrase 'babe-magnet' from Alice and will keep using it.

Alice broke up today, so can utilise her next week for farmers' markets, plus riding course/fishing lake fee collection, having used trip to see Debbie as a bribe. Debbie has promised they'll do Paris, see the sights and lots of shopping. Alice already planning what to pack.

Saturday 12th July

Mum round begging for White Elephant stuff for fête, am sure we have loads, just no time to look it out. While we were having coffee, Adam came in to ring about spare part for one of the tractors. Mum managed to be almost normal with him, definitely melting a bit, so that's something.

Terrible news at Brookfield – two reactors from the test Alistair did last week, their third dose of TB in ten years. Awful bad luck. Jill says David says bad luck, phooey, it's all down to badgers, why has the problem not been addressed by the politicians?

Sunday 13th July

Don't know what new vicar would make of us if today had been his first service: came out of church to find Tom and Kirsty, Will and Emma staggering round village green 'practising' for wife-carrying race, Kirsty hanging upside down with her ankles round Tom's neck like a bat, or possibly some kind of tantric sex position. Meanwhile Jolene informs me Sid's been taking a sack of potatoes with him on his early morning jogs, whilst Eddie has substituted a bag of compost for Clarrie. It's as if Ambridge takes leave of its senses every summer.

Alice at Stables all day: Shula's offered her extra lessons in exchange for help mucking out as one of her girl grooms is off. Since Alice is gearing up for Local Show next Saturday, this is manna (manure?) from heaven. Shula reports Alistair is planning fearsome obstacle course for wife carrying race, clearly he has taken leave of senses too.

Monday 14th July

Debbie rang this evening, could hear fireworks popping in background for Bastille Day, she says they had some magnificent ones at the weekend too. She's been invited to the wedding of one of her colleagues and the christening of another's little boy, both of which she was talking about without any hint of angst. France really seems to have effected complete transformation in her, thank goodness. Asked about farm, harvest, venison, strawberries – hesitate to say it, but quite normal, in fact. Even sent 'regards' to Brian. Thirty-five degrees in Rheims, almost as hot here. After sunniest February since heaven knows when and driest March, warmest June is being followed by seemingly sizzling July.

Things at boiling point at Brookfield certainly, on first day of harvest, Brian absolutely spitting. Over there early, as agreed, but by lunchtime a huge hold-up because Adam's trailer had a puncture which took ages to mend – rusty wheel nuts or something, which of course Brian says should have been checked, taken off and oiled before harvest. Then a problem with the burner at the grain dryer, which meant most of the grain already tipped had to be taken out and the engineer called and so it went on, until Brian refused to leave the combine idle any longer, brought it back here and got on with our barley.

David livid, had the nerve to try and blame Brian for their dryer not working, apparently Debbie used to get it serviced at the same time as ours, as a result it hadn't been done this year. Hardly Brian's fault – as he was quick to point out, there's nothing in the contract about it. Anyway, now he or Adam's got to go back and finish off Brookfield barley sometime, which is an irritant, there's only a tiddly bit left to do. Heigh-ho.

Tuesday 15th July

Alice and I at Hollerton farmers' market – very jolly atmosphere, even Alice enjoyed it – well, didn't complain too much – luckily there was a 'fit' boy on a nearby stall selling ostrich burgers. Took £850! Brian said it quite makes up for hassles yesterday, if we carry on like this he'll put rest of arable into set-aside and sit at home with his feet up while the deer pay our way. Still broiling. Some place in Worcestershire 34 degrees apparently, Borsetshire can't have been far behind.

Thursday 17th July

Spent all morning helping Alice get stuff ready for Pony Club camp next week – Spearmint is taking more luggage than she is. Then off to Stables as had promised would watch her practise jumps for local show on Saturday. Shula says the competition will be stiff, but is confident Alice can hold her own.

Alice, for once not on horseback!

Brenda Tucker has inveigled Adam into a night out tonight with herself, Roy and Hayley in Birmingham – some band in a pub or something. Wouldn't have thought it was Adam's scene, but he seems keen to go, says it will make a change to see bright lights that aren't those of an oncoming combine. They've been harvesting till dark all this week.

Friday 18th July

Adam a bit the worse for wear this morning – not back till nearly two, but had enjoyed himself. Roy and Hayley had to drop out in the end, so it was just him and Brenda: I bet, scheming little minx! Said they went on to a club, had a good time. Still not at all sure about Brenda, after her history with this family, but at least Adam's safe from her wiles!

Saturday 19th July

Local horse show at Worcester: Alice carried off another rosette. Definitely on a roll.

Sunday 20th July

Fête day. Have to say, wife-carrying race was hilarious. Alistair had surpassed himself with the course, which included section of polytunnel and brush jump from riding school – so much so that rest of fête was squashed into end of green nearest Glebelands, to Derek Fletcher's obvious disgust. Mum's White Elephant right next to coconut shy, said she needed hard hat more than wife carrying contestants! Event won by Greg and Helen despite surprisingly good run by Eddie and Clarrie, till he slipped going across pond and put literal damper on their chances. New vicar turned up unannounced, moving in at Darrington properly next weekend. Seems thoroughly nice chap. Daughter not in evidence, but have invited them both to tea Friday week, to long face from Alice. 'Mum, she's probably a total geek.' Not very Christian, as I pointed out to further earful of abuse.

Tuesday 22nd July

First of two farmers' markets this week – we're already expanding! Ruth along to help, and to see how one works from the inside, though she and David are still intending marketing the Herefords through ads in parish magazine. She apologised for David's flying off the handle last week, excuse is he was stressed about the TB. Didn't say anything, but he wants to watch his temper. He's not always the saint everyone makes him out to be.

Markets just get better and better – took over a thousand today! Not all profit, of course, as Brian keeps reminding me, but can tell he's pleased really. Still no chance, though, for he and Adam to have man-to-man chat. Know Adam is starting to feel like I do – things going so well between them, loathe to ruin it. Brian can't sing Adam's praises enough – venison, strawberries, working together really well on harvest, nothing like the strain he thought it'd be without Debbie, Adam has really grown into the role, etc., etc.

Phil round with photos of past fêtes for me to scan in for feature on website. Just shrieking with laughter at some of the clothes – everyone is wearing hats, for a start, as if at Royal Ascot – when phone rang: Lynda Snell to inform me that Foursquare – silent since mid-month – is back on the board!

Wednesday 23rd July

Worked on fête feature for website, logged on to message board. Foursquare on fine form, lengthy postings about fête, indignity of wife carrying, noise, litter, pony droppings, llama droppings, smell of doughnuts/candy floss – better handle would be 'Killjoy'. Lynda still refusing either to reveal his/her identity, or to ban him/her from the board, with result that Joe Grundy is now going around saying she is Foursquare, owing to their long-running vendetta which began with the Open Gardens and has culminated in Joe having to appear before council planning committee next week re: lack of planning permission for pole barn, which may, if they find against him, have to come down. Joe is fighting back with something called the 'Corrugated Iron Club' which promotes corrugated buildings as beautiful and distinctive local architecture. He has insisted I put up a picture of his barn on the website. Had not got energy to resist, though there will doubtless be hell to pay from Lynda. Anyway, feel rather sorry for Grundys. Barn is doing no harm.

Thursday 24th July

Brian knows about Adam. As bad as – no, actually, worse than – I feared.

Day started innocuously enough: Borchester farmers' market, on own for first time as Alice at camp. Market quieter than has been, but guess with schools broken up, some people have already gone away. Mum and Jack called by to say hello, so invited them over for cup of tea this afternoon – again, harmless enough, you'd have thought. Except that, with Mum and I off in the kitchen, Jack, it seems, let slip to Brian about Adam!

Absolute nightmare, though can't blame poor Jack – hardly unreasonable he should expect Brian to be in the know – after all, they've known for a month. Anyway, appears Jack said something to Brian about admiring how well he/we were 'coping' with all the gossip that's circulating about Adam in the village – apparently rife. In fact, now I know the extent of it, realise it's a miracle someone hasn't blurted something out to Brian well before now.

Anyway, the minute Mum and Jack had gone, Brian immediately on to me: why hadn't I told him? A bit taken aback, of course, but replied that it wasn't really my news to broadcast, to which he smartly rejoindered it had been broadcast pretty widely in the village – did the rest of the family know – why had he been left out of the loop? Then all about what an idiot he felt being the last to know, had I any idea what that felt like? Well, actually, yes, I have!! The bloody cheek of the man!! So naturally we had to revisit the Siobhan scenario yet again – how 'out of the loop' did he think I felt after his deception all last year, etc etc. To which he had the nerve to say that this was different, he'd never asked me to live with or work alongside Siobhan, or insinuated her into my life... Could literally feel my jaw dropping – she insinuated herself pretty damn well if you ask me! Couldn't believe his nerve, so ended up having slanging match over that – just, of course, what the relationship experts tell you not to do, bring up past grievances when arguing about something completely different. I'd like to see them try!

No point dwelling on Siobhan, anyway. Back to what's important – Adam. More than my worst fears realised – Brian clearly very, very uncomfortable, to say the least, with fact he is gay – yet vehemently denying he has a problem with it, which makes it even worse. Insists he's not ashamed, it doesn't affect anything, he's just annoyed about the way he had to find out, but know for sure he's not telling the truth. Just know this is going to come between them – and after all Adam's hard work on the farm, after they've been getting on so well. Had sudden, stabbing fear. It took Debbie ages to decide to move on when she found she couldn't live with Brian, but Adam hasn't got her ties to this place, he's used to a rootless life, he could pack up and leave tomorrow.

If Brian's attitude drives Adam away, I really, really will never forgive him. Told him so.

Friday 25th July

Brooded all night. This morning told Brian again that I meant it: he was absolutely not to let this come between him and Adam. And that I hadn't forgotten what happened with Debbie. That obviously struck home. Brian insistent that Adam's being gay makes no difference at all, he's fine about it. Oh, yes, absolutely, which is why he's gone all stiff and formal with of him – spent all lunch talking about the weather, for goodness' sake, when you'd think we've got rather more important things to discuss!

Adam putting on brave face, says it's his own fault for delaying telling Brian. He's told Brian this and apologised, but just got the 'business as usual', no problem at all, line. Then Brian added it would just take him some time to get used to. Which, as Adam points out, means Brian has got a problem with it, because it's either something you accept or you don't. But Adam still insists he's fine, says other friends of his have encountered far worse on coming out to their parents and he'll tough it out.

Have traced gossip back, with Adam's help, to Brenda Tucker. Seems last week when they went out, the club they went on to was a gay club, which was fine, Brenda had been before – have read about this, lots of young women go to gay clubs knowing they can spend the evening unscathed, as it were – but it became clear Adam knew lots of people there and Brenda twigged. Suppose she then spread it around. Feel can't very well ask Jill or Pat what they've heard, and from whom, but have to presume everyone knows – bet it was the talk of the fête! Thought people were giving me funny looks.

Now not sure what to do about telling Alice, due back from Pony Club camp this evening. Adam says she won't give a stuff, she'd probably be more interested to hear Spearmint was gay than him. Doubtless quite true.

Sunday 27th July

Pat on phone at lunchtime to let me know discreetly Adam was being gossiped about in the shop – and to do a bit of even more discreet digging, I suspect. Will be interesting to see if Sid, who was so homophobic over poor Sean, continues to promote Adam for cricket captain. Can only hope he doesn't freeze Adam out, though Adam says he can handle it, he never wanted to be cricket captain anyway. And maybe Jolene's had a civilising effect?

Monday 28th July

Reassuring to know some stereotypes still linger: Lynda accosted Adam today and tried to line him up for her Christmas panto – all her gay friends, she says, are theatrical!

Poor Adam. Has not got a theatrical bone in his body – recall that in school play aged eleven he had such stage fright he delivered his one line from the wings.

Wednesday 30th July

Brookfield's rape and barley finally finished in dribs and drabs. Don't know why Brian's bothered about keeping the wretched contract, it's such a fiddle, but nonetheless much general rejoicing as David's magnanimously decided to keep us on for next year. Had words with Brian, however, when he started moaning this evening about Adam going to nets: 'Debbie would never have done that…' and 'There's always bales to cart…' Told him that if he wanted bales carting he should have said so, not started muttering behind Adam's back. It's incredible how, in less than a week, Adam's gone from being the Boy Wonder to someone who can't do anything right – conversely Debbie, in her absence, is now being idealised as the Golden Girl who could do no wrong. But, of course, it's absolutely nothing at all to do with Adam being gay! Not according to Brian, anyway, who insists nothing has changed. Told him that if that's what he thinks, he should take a long hard look at himself.

The biggest irony of it all is that Brian himself sloped off to the pub after supper to seal the deal with David – and he's announced he's off to the Game Fair at the weekend – as usual, one law for him and another for everybody else. And that's without even mentioning last year, when he was off bonking in Biarritz – sorry, shooting in Scotland – leaving Debbie to cope on her own. Don't know what's more staggering sometimes – his hypocrisy, his arrogance or his inability to see it. Grrr. Public schools have a lot to answer for.

Thursday 31st July

Shula rang to warn me they'd had another horse slashed at the Stables – had managed to keep similar horrid incident a fortnight ago quiet from Alice, but Shula thinks word will get out about this one as was a horse at livery and the owner's (understandably) kicking up a fuss. Poor Shula distraught, both for animal and impact it could have on the business. Had thought first attack was a one-off, but now starting to look as if Stables are being targeted. Such a worry for her. Quite a crime wave in village at present – lots of petty thefts – tools, lawnmowers, etc. – and the other week a central heating boiler and radiators from the showhouse at Grange Spinney.

In fact, atmosphere in Ambridge feels pretty malevolent all round: Foursquare crowing on message board as retrospective planning permission for Joe's barn has been refused – looks as though it will have to come down after all.

Friday 1st August

Brian off early to the Game Fair – picked up by chums from CLA and have checked out where they're staying, so any half-formed fears about reunion with Siobhan over the shooting sticks duly quashed. Neither ashamed nor surprised that I still feel need to check up on him. In fact perfectly logical: if trust takes years to build, how long does it take to rebuild? Realise, as I realised at the time, how very fortunate I am that

194

Siobhan elected to move away – at least don't have to log his mileage every time he goes to the farmers' cash-and-carry – but any longer jaunt still unsettles me. Can't see a time when it won't. What amazes me is how I've assimilated this kind of background uncertainty into my life – hardly even notice it any more. Like scar tissue over a wound I suppose.

Tea here this afternoon with Alan Franks and daughter Amy. Having already met him, nearly fell over when saw her, as she is black! Well, not black, exactly, but mixed race. Having been the first to round on Mum for her prejudices, made me realise how crass and predictable one's assumptions are. Turns out his wife, who died when Amy was only six, was Jamaican. Wondered what on earth Mum, also invited, would make of this, but she is patently so relieved to have a male vicar again she seems willing to forgive him anything. Also we have Lucas in the family now, of course. Anyway, she and Alan got on like a church on fire.

In fact, has been a day of Mum facing down her demons. During baking session with her this morning, in middle of greasing tins, suddenly announced she'd been thinking about things. Presumed she was going to launch into a diatribe about Adam, so tried to cut her off, but she amazed me by bringing up something I'd said to her months ago, when I was really down, about this irrational dread that, should I die before Brian, he could cut my children out of his will and leave the farm and everything else to Ruairi. Was astonished she'd even remembered it. When I said it I was probably just having a bad day, one of those desperate, paranoid moments that I had a lot of in the spring, and I should never have voiced it – certainly not to her, though I never imagined for a moment she'd do anything about it. However, she announced calmly that she's going to open four offshore accounts, one for each of the children, and put money in them! Four: including one for Adam. Very moved – and so was Adam when I told him. A real gesture of reconciliation. So: looks like Mum down, only Brian to go.

Saturday 2nd August

Very warm. 'Heatwave' predicted until at least middle of next week, though Brian, ever the sceptic, says will doubtless follow usual harvest pattern of two fine days and a thunderstorm.

Prompted by weather, Alice agitating to invite Amy Franks for a swim. Came this afternoon. They are already fast friends, helped in no small measure by Amy worshipping horses almost as much as Alice does, and by extension, Alice too. Would be great relief for Alice to have a friend nearby – felt last winter car could have found its own way to Holly's – and, in time, might get us over problem of exercising Chandler who's been getting as fat as butter with only being ridden once or twice a week.

Have been thinking a lot about these offshore accounts of Mum's. In a sense feel a bit guilty – it is in a way a deception of Brian, but on the other hand it wouldn't be happening if he hadn't so comprehensively deceived me. And leaving aside Brian's misdemeanours, it's not as though Mum hasn't got a perfect right – and the money – to do it anyway. It's the sort of thing her accountant might well have advised her to do, whatever.

I suppose I just feel that, while six months ago I might have jumped at the idea, things have moved on. Despite needing to check up that his Game Fair trip was genuine, despite this niggling worry over how he's behaving towards Adam, I can't help feeling that Brian and I have made progress. It's so odd. I spent so long at the beginning of the year wondering how long it would take to feel 'normal' again – wondering if I ever would – but there's actually something about this thing over Adam which feels very 'normal' – me having to intercede on behalf of one of the children against Brian's entrenched position. It was the same at the end of term with Alice's exam results and the time she was spending on the horses. Or, equally, like that business with her pierced belly button, it might just as well be the other way round, with me the one who needed to be talked round.

What it actually means, when you look at it, is Brian and I reacting like any parents – like any couple – not always in agreement, but subtly working on each other till some kind of accommodation's reached. I suppose what I'm saying is that we seem to have fallen back into our old way of life – which may seem like nothing but friction, but in the end is exactly what 'normal' life's about – coping with the little daily niggles – and the bigger things – by what might seem like simply muddling through, or half the time, in this family at least, lurching from crisis to crisis! But feeling that beneath the surface there's a well that can be drawn on – a well of... I'm not sure what. A shared purpose? A commonality? A communality? Mutual respect? Trust, even? Maybe it's no more than history and habit. But I can only think it's what sustains you when everything else has withered away and which, eventually, encourages and enables it to grow back.

It seems to have got us this far, anyway.

Sunday 3rd August

Bishop Cyril here for Alan's induction service. Tempted to ask him where he stood on the gay bishop saga both here and in USA but thought better of it: enough controversy on the subject in my own family. As is the custom, Alan tolled the bell after the service – if, as tradition dictates, number of rings is a measure of the length of his incumbency, we can expect eight years, which should see Alice through, anyway. She and Amy have really taken to each other.

Brian not in best of tempers as with the strawberries coming on line next week, Adam's going to be occupied with them pretty much full time for the next month or so. Their ripening can hardly have come as a surprise and Adam's lined up pickers and everything but Brian will keep moaning we're back to square one despite having taken on a student for harvest, i.e. minus a driver for the grain trailers. Also creating merry hell about the fact that the pickers – students, mostly, camping – are going to have to use the downstairs shower room. Keep telling him we have to adopt blitz spirit. It's not as if he ever uses it and anyway, if he's as busy as he says he is, he won't be around to let them doing so bother him, will he?!

Monday 4th August

After all Brian's huffing and puffing, Mike Tucker jumped at the chance to come and help out grain-hauling. Brian also tried to enlist him in this farm watch which he, Tony and David are masterminding in response to all the thefts locally. Alistair keen to be involved too. Brian a bit despondent about Farm Watch in general, though: some people muttering about 'vigilantes'. Adam thinks they'd be better off using the website or e-mail to tip people off: like the 'snow spider' system they use at Alice's school. More work, but said I'd chat to Usha about it: no good calling for Blitz spirit, then not putting best foot forward and other such cliches. Granny P. would be proud of me.

Tuesday 5th August

First of three farmers' markets this week, selling strawberries as well as venison. Broiling weather still and they went like hot – well, strawberries. Thought people might be fed up with them this late in the year, but fact they are English and local triumphs over everything. Plus had two different varieties which people could sample before buying. Still finding markets great fun, not sure how I'll cope though when Alice is in France – only ten days to go now, as she will keep reminding me.

Mysterious shift in Brian's attitude towards Adam, who reports that on finding Ed and Jazzer strawberry-picking, some of the other pickers having not turned up, Brian utterly failed to give Adam the expected bollocking – instead squeezed out something resembling an apology, admitting harvest staffing situation hardly Adam's fault as when the strawberries were planted, none of us had any idea Debbie would be in France. Adam reckons a touch of the sun is responsible. Can think of no other explanation – but good!

Thursday 7th August

First chance this week to get on computer and tidy up website. Glanced at message board, only to see posting accusing David of shooting a badger and asking since when have parish councillors been allowed to 'flout the law of the land'. Astonished, but rang Jill and she confirms it's true: what's worse, the RSPCA may prosecute.

It's all Matt Crawford's fault apparently, he saw David dumping the body and reported him out of spite because the PC opposed his 'mansion' plan. That man. If he lived in the village I'd be convinced he was Foursquare. Mind you, David does act first, think later, as Brian will testify with all that fuss over the grain dryer/our contract the other week. Brian, however, sympathetic to David on this one: says he'd personally shoot every badger in the country if he could. Many farmers might agree, but nonetheless pointed out it is against the law. Brian just gave me a withering look and said if on side of cuddly animals how did I justify buying those fur-lined gloves in Hungary? And was I really going to say no to Mum's mink hat when she dies? It's a good job I love him as his insistence on always having the last word is the most infuriating thing I know.

Friday 8th August

Back exhausted from Felpersham Farmers' Market, heat almost intolerable and Alice very little help as kept sloping off to look at the shops. She is insistent on having all new stuff for France: keep trying to point out Debbie's making the ultimate sacrifice and taking her shopping in Paris but Alice says not the point: in her ancient (i.e. month-old) trainers, assistants will give her pitying glances and, what's worse, no boy will give her a second look. In end gave up, gave her £30 out of cash box, told her to come back with a smile on her face. And shoes, not trainers. She returned, beaming, with glittery flip-flops.

Saturday 9th August

Amy over for ride and swim: told Alice to play down all these new clothes she's having. Alan's told Shula straight out that riding lessons for Amy are beyond his budget, so Shula's got her mucking out in exchange for the odd hack.

Harvest going well, strawberries going well, though – poor Adam – pickers deeply unreliable. Brian relieved now Farm Watch is off his back and on to mine. Police are going to send me details of suspicious characters in vicinity, recent thefts reported, etc., and I'm to circulate to everyone who's registered their e-mail address with our Farm Watch scheme. Am doing it for now, but have cunning plan to offload onto Ruth before long.

Sunday 10th August

Curmudgeon in Brian surfaced again when heard William and Emma have got engaged: hopes they won't be expecting a present. Agree, but must surely send a card. If it hadn't been for William, how would Brian have coped with Greg's absences this year? His elder girl Sonja arrives today for a holiday – according to Pat, the teenager from hell, via Marseilles.

Think may have found reason for Brian's seeming thaw towards Adam. Sorting through suitcases in loft – though steamer trunk wouldn't be big enough for amount she wants to take – when Alice said something about Amy finding it 'cool' that she had a brother who was gay. (Adam apparently having told Alice the other week). Added, however, that she'd had to tell Brian off for being so 'prattish' about it before he showed himself up in front of her friends. Can't imagine Brian cares what the likes of Amy Franks thinks, but there are plenty of other people in front of whom he wouldn't want to lose face. Whatever. Good for Alice!

Tuesday 12th August

Glorious 12th. Poor, poor Clarrie. When I last saw her she was floating on air about William and Emma: now it turns out that Ed's been caught red-handed burgling a house – or rather, a garage – up at Warren

Coppice. Brian hit the roof – on Sunday morning, by agreement with Adam, Ed and Jazzer had only been selling strawberries for us at a car boot! Now Brian says neither of them is ever setting foot on this farm again. (Have heard it all before, of course). Ed, it seems, was at Magistrates' Court this morning, guilty plea entered, adjourned for four weeks for police reports, probation reports, pre-sentence reports and the rest. Bailed and under curfew apparently though this still not enough for Brian who says Ed should be electronically tagged.

Amy over for the afternoon, overheard her and Alice speculating that Ed could be the one slashing horses. Can't believe it of him – Oliver always maintains he's got a real feel for stock – but seems when he was caught he was stealing knives and a set of chisels. Don't like the sound of it. And dreading what Foursquare will have to say. So far this month he's been preoccupied, predictably enough, apart from ongoing pole barn rantings, with slow-moving harvest traffic.

wednesday 13th August

Farmers' market with Alice. Began well enough but had to have strict word when she started going on again about Ed and the horse slashings – she may be a minor but she needs to grasp the laws of slander. Further fell out when informed her had agreed to have Greg's hell-child Sonja over on Friday – Helen rang last night sounding so desperate, hadn't the heart to refuse and frankly, with a dozen or more strawberry-pickers traipsing through the house the whole time, one more hardly makes any difference. Alice in a sulk, however, having wanted to spend the last afternoon before her holiday communing with Spearmint, Amy and Chandler. Then had the cheek to demand I take her to Felpersham tomorrow (the one day of the week I was hoping not to drive anywhere as have no Farmers' Market to do) as she's decided she wants the special ceramic hair straighteners after all which you can't get in Borchester. Bound to blow France's national grid with them. Must get her an adaptor plug.

Thursday 14th August

Brian flat out on harvest, the minute he finishes our second wheats it's over to Brookfield, plus other odd bits of contract work. Reminded him it could be worse: it was this time last year that we had the combine fire, then realised how foolish I was, as that was the lead-up to his week's so-called shooting – in fact his liaison in Biarritz. However, instead of letting our eyes slide away from each other, and a deathly silence falling, he looked straight at me, paused, said that was a good point, he should count his blessings: he wouldn't want to go through last year again. Said quietly I wouldn't either.

Another fortnight gone by on fast-forward since I last stopped and thought about 'Brian and I'. Am confirmed in my suspicion that, seemingly without any conscious effort on either of our parts, we have entirely slipped back into the consoling rhythm of 'normal life' that everyone talks about, the life you don't give a thought to while you're living it, and the one that, if you did, would seem so humdrum, but by contrast, when your life's been turned upside down, becomes the most desirable and unattainable thing in the world.

Just so grateful not to be upside down any more.

Friday 15th August

9.30 a.m. As if haven't got enough to think about, Adam has had bright idea of a barbecue for the strawberry pickers this evening – Brian in favour 'pour encourager les autres', not that he'll have to do the shopping. Actually quite excited, love imagining myself as fixed point at centre of whirlwind that is harvest time, and Brian says am at my best when feeding minimum 5000. Off to supermarket.

11 p.m. Whirlwind more like eye of storm. Day dominated by fluctuating hormones, mostly teenage, some of them mine.

At three on the dot – the appointed hour, they must have been waiting at the bottom of the drive – Helen dropped off a very surly Sonja, most inappropriately clad for the afternoon Alice had planned i.e. veneration of Spearmint. Must have been seven o'clock, barbecue in full swing, before I realised hadn't seen Sonja for hours. Challenged Alice who said she thought she'd gone home! At first cross with Alice and Amy whom I assumed had frozen her out, then very embarrassed as when rang Greg to apologise, the wretched girl wasn't there either – seems we'd lost her! Have to say he was remarkably phlegmatic, didn't seem exactly surprised, just said he'd drive around a bit and look for her. Though barbecue itself a great success, somewhat tense evening as a result.

Finally got a call from Greg at half ten to say Sonja had shown up back at his place, then further furtive call from Helen ten minutes ago apologising to me for Sonja's behaviour and offering to pay for the wine! (Turns out the little madam had taken a bottle from the barbecue table and gone and drunk most of it by the lake!) Hope this is not the sort of behaviour that Alice will think is clever when she comes back from France.

Oh, yes, and my hormones. This morning met Jill in supermarket, learnt by the by that Elizabeth's gone to Ireland for a couple of days to see Siobhan. Poor Jill so artless, prattling on, had to occupy self as if debating between pasta twists or bows but awful plunging lift-in-stomach feeling came back just like beginning of year. And when had so thought all that was over. Suppose it was just because was a reminder that she hasn't really gone that far away – and perhaps that once Siobhan Hathaway checks into your life, she never really checks out.

Brian calling me to come to bed. Suspect this is not with seduction in mind but because we have to be up at six to get Alice to airport. Oh well. The difference, I suppose, between being the mistress and the wife.

Saturday 16th August

Just back from Birmingham, having waved off frighteningly confident Alice on her solo flight. House seems very quiet. Helen round with bunch of flowers apologising again for Sonja's behaviour yesterday – poor thing looks exhausted, says she's not sure how they're going to get through another week.

Sunday 17th August

Alice rang last night, full of Paris – have feeling Debbie not quite sure if she's going to get through a week with a teenager either.

Brian and Adam harvesting at Brookfield so took self off to mum's for the day – luckily Ruth fed Brian at lunchtime – or not so luckily, in his view, as he had to force down shop-bought steak pie, frozen peas and microwaved baked potato – all high on his list of top ten food hates of all time. Says he doesn't know how David does a day's work on what

Ruth feeds him which I suppose is an indirect compliment. Had only intended something salady tonight but (possibly still haunted by mention of Siobhan on Friday) got trout out of freezer and made quick pâté followed by venison steaks. Was appreciated. Strawberries (yawn) for pudding – have tons to eat. Threat of rain next week – having heard forecast, Adam had to ring pickers and tell them not to bother coming in tomorrow. Plus threat of botrytis hanging over us. Brian nobly saying nothing.

Monday 18th August

Debbie rang to report on Parisian progress – very wisely made Alice do the sights Saturday afternoon, knowing that once exposed to the shops there'd be no looking back. Galeries Lafayette, Printemps, Kookai, Zara all done yesterday, apparently – Debbie on her knees. Today's agenda is the designer shops (just looking) and photos in front of the Georges V – Alice has pretended they're staying there to make Holly jealous. Debbie says clear that Alice's dominant gene (shopping) inherited from me – on same basis that playing babies Mozart in womb makes them classical music lovers, blames all the time I spent browsing in Underwoods when pregnant. But she's clearly loving having Alice there.

Am missing her – was tough today doing Farmers' Market on my own. Also got to do one Wednesday.

Wednesday 20th August

Thank God Adam and Brian are getting on better – international incident narrowly averted today when Brian found Ed Grundy here strawberry-picking. Adam says he was desperate for labour, and, rather like me, hadn't believed Brian's ultimatum the other week, but Brian actually threw Ed off the farm. Oliver on phone this evening remonstrating with Brian – 'Give the boy a chance', etc – Brian says if Oliver had known the Grundys as long as he has, and had seen the endless chances people have given them, he would be rather less magnanimous. Can't help feeling sorry for them, though – it's all bad news at the moment. Seems Joe has now had official letter from council ordering him to take down the pole barn and 'restore the land to its original condition'. Brian says does this mean tidy up the field, as Grundys have littered it with bits of old machinery, bags of compost, etc., but since was formerly rank mess of weeds and thistles, am not sure what is worse.

Friday 22nd August

Badger saga also rumbles on: poor David apparently got a pasting from Derek Fletcher at Parish Council meeting. As David's still on tenterhooks about a possible prosecution, just what he doesn't need. George is in despair: having just got someone onto the PC who's lowered the average age by about fifty years, the last thing he wants is for David to resign.

Message board has been vile recently, what with Foursquare gloating both about the 'badger-slayer' and the pole barn coming down. Have asked Lynda outright if Foursquare is Derek Fletcher but she's still hiding behind this confidentiality nonsense, which only confirms my suspicions, as both she and Derek are anti-pole barn and, presumably, pro-wildlife – not that you'd think it from the amount of slug pellets I saw him liberally sprinkling round his bizzie-lizzies the other day. Anyway, seems Joe is going to appeal about his barn: if he comes round here asking for support am going to give it to him, apart from anything else out of sheer bloody-mindedness towards Lynda and Derek – when I think of the torment that man put me through all winter with his tedious e-mails… When said this at supper, however, Brian roundly declared that if I support the Grundys he'll divorce me. Could hear Adam holding his breath – had Brian gone too far? – but I just laughed, so we all did.

Saturday 23rd August

Alice back from France absolutely exhausted, though not as exhausted as Debbie I would guess, who must be flat broke but will return to work complete with raft of new clothes selected by Alice, who reports she's given her a 'total makeover'. Have to say, probably long overdue, clothes shopping not Debbie's strong point. Alice herself sporting new top (one of three bought her by Debbie), has also bought (incredibly sensibly) pea-coat for winter, inevitable jeans, and vast freight of make-up, hair bobbles, etc. Some of it, though, presents for friends, including Amy Franks, which is sweet. Brought – well, smuggled, I suppose – bottle of Bordeaux for Brian and for me some wonder-gel that's supposed to remove cellulite – 'Well, you're always moaning about it, Mum'. Kind thought I suppose, if hardly tactful. Lovely to have her back though, and wonderful to see her photos of Debbie looking so well. Rapturous reunion for Alice with Spearmint, who got bag of French mint imperials.

Monday 25th August

Lower Loxley had Country Fayre on so went over with Alice for couple of hours. Usual stalls, crafts, etc. Nigel seems very taken with his green woodworking – has now made two stools and is working on a chair – as if they need any more furniture in that place, ecologically sound or not!

Had little pang as suddenly remembered it was Bank Holiday last year that we had them over to dinner with the phantom grouse Brian had supposedly shot, and what an awkward evening that was. Now of course know why – Elizabeth must have known all about Siobhan and Brian's tryst in Biarritz. Felt a bit low, then pulled self together – reminded self should feel triumphant – but was suddenly desperately curious to know what's become of her.

Couldn't ask Elizabeth, so when got home rang Jill and casually dropped it into conversation, said had forgotten to ask Elizabeth, how had her visit to Ireland gone? Seemingly Siobhan still in Dublin, though not with mother any more, is renting house. Working freelance when she can around the baby, who apparently is lovely, though teething. Took me back to my time in Bristol with Adam – the nightmare of that first winter, dropping him off at childminder, teaching all day, shopping on way back home, heating up his bottles and baby rice on the gas ring in that dismal bedsit, evenings spent preparing next day's lessons – shudder to think of it.

Wonder if Ruairi still looks like Alice when she was a baby – or if he's starting to look like his father? Pointless to speculate. Will never know – nor, hopefully, will Brian. Still hate thinking about the whole thing – feel so angry, sad, resentful – expect she feels the same. And Brian too, sometimes. What he's given up. Extraordinary.

Felt ridiculously tender towards him as a result. This evening massaged his neck for ages, stiff from looking over his shoulder on combine.

Jennifer's Diary

Wednesday 27th August

Another attack at the stables last night – on Caroline's horse, Moonlight
– well, actually he was Guy's horse, which is somehow even worse – and
he's had to be put down. Alice beside herself, says she won't be able to
sleep till whoever's doing this is caught. Still whisperings in the village
it's Ed Grundy, but the police aren't linking the crimes – not yet, anyway.
Really can't believe it of Ed, though Brian just gives his smug look and
keeps saying 'shades of Alf'. Pointed out that Alf Grundy was never
charged with anything more serious than handling stolen copper wire,
at least as far as I know. Brian says that was a long time ago, who knows
what he's been doing since? I retorted that for all we knew he'd
reformed in prison, found God, discovered poetry, whatever. Brian
snorted, asked if I'd seen the moisture meter, and went out to help Adam
skin a deer. Honestly, sometimes feels like redneck country round here:
Borsetshire would be perfect location for one of those films where
hapless couple's car breaks down and they are offered help by wild-eyed
locals who then dismember them in woods.

Alice took card round to Caroline saying how sorry we all are. Tried to
phone Shula to say the same but got answering machine.

Friday 29th August

Met Shula at shop – she looks so ill. Says she hasn't slept properly since all
this started – six weeks ago, now – and feels terrible about Caroline. Police
still have no leads, though they've now interviewed Ed. Inconclusive all
round: he may be under curfew, but how can he prove he was in bed at
four o'clock in the morning or whenever it happened? Pat says Clarrie
looks terrible too. Message board alive with it all – truly horrible. Alice
checking on Chandler, Spearmint and Tolly every minute of the day.

On top of this, farmer's markets seem like light relief. Harvest pretty much over and (to a mere – yet eloquent – raised eyebrow from Brian) Adam has put ads in papers and on Radio Borsetshire for PYO this weekend as supply of pickers has all but dried up. Has done signs, borrowed scales and taken advice from Mike and Neil (was pretty much 'don't bother' but Adam hasn't told Brian that obviously) so we shall just have to see.

Somehow feel that the summer which started with such high drama – Debbie, Adam – is petering out somewhat with dribs and drabs of harvest, strawberries and unsettled feel in village. Don't like this whole Ed/horse-slashing thing, don't like thefts, don't like Foursquare, don't like idea that Matt Crawford is taking over Ambridge (Grange Spinney, his 'mansion' plan which he's clearly going to carry on resubmitting till he gets it through – and now he's buying Nightingale Farm – why?? – to knock it down and build his mansion there? All very worrying). And then there's Brookfield, another TB test hanging over them next week and still not knowing if David's going to be prosecuted over the badger.

But then... when I look back at my diary for this time last year, it's unbelievable, really: in its innocence, almost wilfully obtuse. All that stuff about feeling sorry for Siobhan – her 'grim flat', her lack of support, the similarity between us (!) in refusing to name the baby's father.

But in a way I still do feel sorry for her. She's clearly not happy – perhaps she never will be. And it's true that we have got a lot in common, the chief thing being that, like it or not, we both seem to be the type that needs a man – sadly, in our case, the same one. She's a generation away from me, but hers is the famously confused Bridget Jones generation, which women of my age automatically envy when we shouldn't really. Her generation may have evolved from mine, yet in so many ways they're just the same, and in others, seem even worse off. Look how obsessed they are with their biological clocks, how they drink to excess and burn themselves out. At Christmas I thought Siobhan was so strong, such a survivor, but now I think that, like me, the whole the time she was just clinging to the wreckage. And now there's nothing for her to cling to.

So all in all, perhaps I should be grateful that the only troubles I've got to think about as this summer fades away are external ones.

RETRIBUTION

Friday 5th September

Haven't felt inspired to write diary all week as 'petering out' feeling persisted. PYO a moderate success... Adam/Brian taking the odd shift on Farm Watch... cultivations coming along... lent digital camera to Joe so he could take photos of his pole barn with its new painted roof... tried to get Alice to do her holiday homework and see my point of view on suitability of new school shoes... life drifting on, in other words. Then, last night, suddenly, full-on drama at the Stables when Neil, on Farm Watch, came face to face with the horse slasher, who is... Clive Horrobin! (This is so typical of Ambridge. The minute you decide you're time-warped in a sleepy sort of 'Brigadoon', reality comes along and bites you on the nose.)

Village today in a ferment: feel desperately sorry for Susan, of course, but most people, Brian amongst them, think they should lock Clive up and, this time, throw away the key. Took Alice over to Stables this afternoon

for a lesson – poor Shula's having to maintain 'business as usual' front –
but she and Alistair are mystified as to why Clive should have targeted
them – unless, Shula was speculating, it's some obscure grudge against
the legal profession going back to when she was married to Mark??
Brian says a no-good like Clive doesn't need an excuse, except, no
doubt, that 'society is to blame', though Adam, instinctively more liberal,
pointed out that the brutalising effect of prison on already disaffected
young men only makes things worse.

Thursday 11th September

Took Alice for riding lesson. Shula trying hard to build up livery side
again – now she can say horse-slashing culprit has been caught, is hopeful
some of her more loyal customers will return. And she's still trying to
come to terms with fact that Clive, it now emerges, had got the wrong
people all along: thought George, whom he blames for his last
incarceration, still lived at the Stables! Shula, though of course glad in a
sense the violence wasn't actually directed at her, is worried for Chris and
George – if Clive has a vendetta against him, how far is he capable of
taking it? No one has any idea of how long he'll be put away for this
time: Susan, poor thing, seems to have latched onto the idea that Clive is
disturbed (some story about him having had a tough time in prison:
knifed or assaulted or something) – though as Brian (yet again) says,
having had one bad experience, Clive should logically want not to
commit a crime which would send him back there again. Adam says that's
the point: someone like Clive, mentally ill or not, does not think logically.

Which is borne out, in fact, by Ed Grundy: his case was up before the
magistrates yesterday. You'd have thought after the shock of that car crash
and what happened to Emma Carter – and what could have happened –

he'd have wanted to stay on the right side of the law, but no. Another community punishment and rehabilitation order – but poor Clarrie apparently just relieved it wasn't a custodial sentence. How does she cope?

Friday 12th September

Not sure if in defiance or celebration of Ed's conviction, but the Grundys are planning a barbecue in their field, to which the whole village appears to be invited, as long as they bring their own drink, and possibly food as well. Ostensibly the reason is Joe's 82nd birthday, but it is in fact a transparent plug for the pole barn and why it should stay. Have to say they have made enormous difference by tidying up the field and of course painting the roof. Not sure, however, if I shall dare to show my face as Lynda is still on the warpath about the barn and I do find strained relations with her – well, a strain, especially as I have to have so much to do with her re: the website and message board. Foursquare's choleric outpourings continue on every subject under the sun and, bizarrely to me, she still continues to protect his/her identity.

Have realised end-of-August lull was nothing more than usual pre-term end-of-August lull: now schools are back (even Alice), pace is picking up again, and certainly village social life. Flower and Produce is on 28th: highlights this year include 'An Unusual Marmalade' and men-only cake is to be Lemon Drizzle. May enter a few flowers or an arrangement, but it's bad timing for me with Alice's birthday the next day: if weather forecast looks good she may well have a sleepover here on the Saturday and swimming party/barbecue on the Sunday. Or pizza/video/sleepover if wet. Either way, doubt if much sleep will be got by any of us. Brian says sleepover, in teenage hands, is the biggest misnomer in the world. He still seems rather grumpy and out-of-sorts: suppose he is tired as, though grain harvest is over, still got beet to lift and, of course, next year's crops to get in. And Adam is still nagging him about strawberries.

Tried to cheer him up by telling him about Harvest Home planned for October 3rd and to be held, this year, in barn at Brookfield, which seems fitting as it is also Jill's birthday. He simply retorted 'What barn?' and expressed marked reluctance to spend, as he put it, 'all evening crouched on a hay bale in their machinery shed with the wind whistling round my ears'. Even promised appearance of Jolene and The Midnight Walkers failed to alter his mood. He'll come round in the end, though. He always does.

Took present round to Brookfield for Josh's birthday – he'll be six tomorrow, incredible. David's still waiting to hear if he's going to be prosecuted over the badger, but at least their latest TB test was clear – and the first beef from their Herefords will be ready for sale next week.

Saturday 13th September

Alice stayed over at Amy Franks' last night and returned with exciting news that a crack has appeared in the living room wall – or, rather, must have been there ages, but has got bigger since they moved in. Can believe this, as Janet was many things, but house-proud not one of them. Alan is reporting to diocese: Alice promptly offered Amy she could move in with us if they have to vacate house while it's fixed! As sounds like subsidence, could be lengthy stay: can imagine what Brian would say to effectively an ongoing 'sleepover' at ours, plus he is not well disposed towards Alan at present as says he's the one who's filled Alice's head with notions of iniquities of global superpowers, free markets, etc, and swung her in favour of fair trade.

Sunday 14th September

Alan gave us all something to think about at church when he asked us to pray for 'families in difficulties' – clearly thinking of the Horrobins – and this after his sermon on forgiveness the other week. Could see even Shula having a bit of trouble with her responses and there were a few raised eyebrows afterwards, especially from George. He wants to borrow a trailer from us on Friday as he plans to clear some of the scrub from the Millennium Wood – said I might even go and give him a hand and would try to get Brian along, too. Would do us good to do something together, especially as he seems to feel generally unloved at the moment, convinced that Adam and Alice are aligned against him on this fair trade argument. Forebore from mentioning that Alan is suggesting using fairly traded as well as locally produced goods for the Harvest Home: can imagine Brian's face when confronted with sun-dried mango and raisins instead of salted peanuts and Pringles. Not to mention the 'fairly traded' wine!

2 p.m. Adam and Alice against him? – add to that list Kate. Was minding my own business at the riding course when Brian suddenly appeared, flourishing an e-mail from her informing us that with the money Mum's put in the offshore fund, she and Lucas are thinking of buying a house – and informing Brian, by the by, about the existence of the fund! Caught completely on the hop, had to burble something about how yes, Mum had given Kate money, but didn't bring up that it was a fund, still less mention that she'd done the same for all the children. Brian clearly thought it very odd, but as needed to buy time to think about how I'm going to tell him, if I'm going to tell him, tried to distract him with prattle about loan of trailer on Friday and would Brian come and help? Be sure your sins will find you out, as they say. Now have to decide what to do.

217

Monday 15th September

Awful – like Adam being gay row all over again, but much, much worse, because I really am at fault this time.

In kitchen making lunch, unaware of hell about to break loose, when Brian came in from the yard. Seems he'd mentioned Kate and Lucas's house purchase plans, and Adam, assuming he therefore knew about all the offshore trusts, said how generous it was of Mum to do the same for all of them. Which it is, Brian assured me. So why hadn't I mentioned it? Absolutely floundering, didn't know what to say. Stupidly tried to pretend she'd only done it for tax purposes and that she could do what she liked with her money – though could see he'd already worked out exactly what the motivation was and knew I must be behind it. Obviously very hurt. Clearly, he said coldly, the implication was that he's not to be trusted to look after the children financially – or in any other way. And, of course, feeling guilty, I foolishly turned defensive.

Dreadful, dreadful scene ensued – still shaking when I think about it, because has potential to undermine everything we've been working towards for the past nine months, which is exactly what Brian said at the end of it. If, he said, I had so little faith in the marriage that I'd allowed financial contingency plans to be set up behind his back, what else might he expect? Had I perhaps got a little or not-so-little fund of my own? As a precursor to leaving him perhaps? Completely and utterly flabbergasted – and, by now, furious – said of course I wasn't going to leave him and the funds were for the children's future security, not mine! But, frankly, anything I said a waste of time by then.

I could see from his eyes how much I'd hurt him – as much as when I accused him of his driving Debbie away during the row about Adam being gay, which I didn't mean, of course – it just came out. And now all this about the trust funds has come out, and in such a senseless, stupid, underhand sort of way! Wish to goodness I'd never said anything to Mum about Brian leaving everything to Ruairi, wish she'd never brooded about it, still less done anything about it – but if all those things had to happen, and did, then so wish I'd found some way to explain it to Brian. Which is a stupid wish in itself. If I could have talked to him – which, actually, Mum always told me to do – if I could have talked to him about my fears for the future and my children's future, none of this would have happened. If only I'd been honest with him… which is what Brian ended up saying. If in the past nine months we haven't learnt to be open and honest with each other, then what have they been for?

Feel absolutely crushed. I'm such an idiot. I don't know how I thought I was going to keep Brian from knowing about these funds anyway and now they've achieved the complete opposite of what I intended. He might now well take the view that since, thanks to Mum, my children are handsomely provided for, he jolly well will leave everything to Ruairi! Wouldn't that just serve me right!

The frustration of it – I could scream. I don't really believe that everything we've worked at together is threatened – don't I? – if I'm honest ? – no, I don't. I still think, like I've always thought – or perhaps I mean hoped – that Brian's got too much invested here, both financially and emotionally, to break it all up. What I do know is that this will set us back. I don't know how far exactly, but I know I've got ground to make up. I'm going to have to work as hard to win Brian round as he did with me at the start of the year. I ranted on enough then about loss of trust:

well, he doesn't trust me right now, and frankly why should he? And what's even worse, he doesn't trust me to trust him, which really is what we've been supposed to be working towards — and where we've made progress, we really have. Or had.

It's such a mess. A setback, and a big one, I know. Bigger even than it looks.

Tuesday 16th September

Brian hardly speaking to me. All overtures rebuffed. Also very gruff with Adam re: a meeting Adam's set up about expanding the strawberries next year. Brian off partridge shooting for the day tomorrow which, under the circumstances, will be a relief.

Learnt in shop that Clive has been remanded for a further three weeks by magistrates while they prepare a pre-sentence report. Susan still pushing for psychiatric report on him but can't see her getting anywhere. Tried this as conversational tack with Brian as criminal classes usually guaranteed to get him going: even this didn't work. Perhaps even more ground to make up than I thought.

Wednesday 17th September

Brian back late from shoot: went to office, then after supper bath and bed; said he was tired. Wanted to talk to him — had been planning all day what to say — but now will have to wait. May not do any harm as what I have to say — apology about trusts of course, and my part in them — could still do with a bit of polishing. Also, as of tonight have had new idea. Am hatching plan which will show him how much value I place on the effort he's put into the family over the past nine months and which will also consolidate us as couple. Needs more research — will do on internet tomorrow.

Thursday 18th September

Brian busy on farm all day, seemed very distracted when came in. At first thought improvement on usual terseness, but continued unexplained all evening. Not sure why, would have probed, but too busy having tussle with Alice over computer. She decided to look up Horse of the Year Show – as a treat, Shula and Alistair are taking her and Amy on Saturday – just as I'd finally found a moment to sit down and look into my new idea. (Sent her off to do it on her computer – so what if her screen's only 15″ ?)

Anyway, my idea is a holiday for me and Brian, which, making a point, I'll pay for out of my savings – partly to mark his 60th, which is coming up in November, but more specifically to say I do have faith in our relationship. South Africa, to see Kate and Lucas, would be the obvious choice. We could either go just the two of us, which would make it more special for us as a couple – or could take Alice, and – this is the clever thing – wondered if I could persuade Debbie to come over as well? Rather proud of this bit, especially as neutral territory would be marvellous way of getting Brian and Debbie together. Now she seems so much happier cannot see that she could object. Also this would leave Adam in charge of farm which would confirm something about his position here.

We had such fun when Brian took up flying. Hope we'll soon be jetting off again!

The more I think about it, the more I'm convinced this is an excellent idea. Would love to see Kate, Lucas and not-so-little Nolly again – photos just aren't the same. Anyway, am going to keep thinking it through.

I want to have all my arguments marshalled when I broach it with Brian. Don't want to be caught on the back foot again, like Monday. This is important. I've got to get it right.

10 p.m. Brian has just poked head round door to say he is going to bed as has big day tomorrow. Gave strange sort of half-grin then disappeared before I could ask him what – surely clearing Millennium Wood can't be that hard if there are plenty of us?

Friday 19th September

Totally wrong in assumption about Millennium Wood. Just because Brian hadn't actually refused, had assumed he was OK to help, but when mentioned it at breakfast, he said not to be ridiculous, he was far too busy this afternoon and he wasn't aware he'd ever committed himself to anything. Technically true, but was slightly taken aback, not to say disappointed: had thought afternoon in fresh air, working alongside each other, would be perfect opportunity to broach holiday idea. Now not to be.

Talk about boot being on other foot! Have appreciated in a small way this week how he must have felt earlier this year when I rebuffed all his attempts at reconciliation – not to mention how Debbie must have made him feel. Still, he persevered, so suppose I must. Smiled sweetly, said it didn't matter, if he had other things to do he must do them. He just grunted and went out to weigh some lambs.

Spent rest of morning feeling wifely and virtuous, making fresh tomato and basil soup for lunch, only to learn from Adam when I went out with coffee that Brian had jumped in the car ten minutes earlier and roared off somewhere – said he wouldn't be back till about five!

Adam had the coffee anyway – and enjoyed the soup – though he's pretty fed up with Brian, who apparently turned up so late yesterday for the strawberry pow-wow Adam's been waiting for all week as to render the whole thing useless. So Adam still doesn't feel he's had chance to put his case. Told him he has to see it from Brian's point of view: since all this offshore thing, Brian obviously feels both vulnerable and slighted – not a good combination when Adam's asking him to invest a load more money to expand next year.

Couldn't resist telling Adam about my holiday idea. He was all for it, and the more I think about it, the more enthused I get. If this holiday doesn't convince Brian that I trust him, that I want to be with him, that I think our future together is both as a couple and a unit, a family – then what will?

10 p.m. Brian back in very strange mood: pleasant, but again distracted, somehow. Better than grumpy, anyway. Proposed evening of TV and bottle of wine, but he apologised very sweetly, said if he was going to do Adam's ideas for strawberries justice, he should spend evening thinking about future of entire farm: would I mind if he shut himself away in office? As was for Adam's sake didn't feel I could say no. Instead took self off and sorted through wardrobe, thinking about holiday: thank goodness bought new swimsuit this summer but wish I'd bought that cream linen outfit with the long loose overshirt in Underwoods' sale. Would have been perfect. Anyway, evening passed very pleasantly and when looked in just now to offer Brian a hot drink he seemed very conciliatory. Think perhaps storm over offshore trusts has passed. In a sense, feel have got off lightly.

Jennifer's Diary

Saturday 20th September

Adam and Brian busy all day getting on with cultivating and drilling. Adam says Brian's in a dream: nearly tipped a whole dumpy bag of seedcorn over yard instead of into drill! Joked with Brian at lunchtime about being past it: he gave a wry smile, said somehow he didn't think so. Told him I didn't think so either.

Their being busy, though, gave me chance to get on website and tidy it up: not sure what to do about it when we are away – am already assuming we're going! – think might ask Usha if she'd take it over. Checked message board and felt had to have a word with Lynda: Foursquare had posted something quite vile about 'criminal tendency' in Ambridge, way beyond his usual 'hang 'em and flog 'em' line. To my relief/amazement, Lynda agreed with me and said she's going to do something about it. Not before time!

Sunday 21st September

Alan is courting controversy again: has moved the church history boards to make way for a leaflet stand plugging Fair Trade and overseas charities. A bit of muttering from Bert. Amy's a very nice girl, though: very grounded, a steadying influence on Alice. She stayed over last night but typically they weren't ready to come down to church with me, so Brian brought them down for the end of the service. In a complete reversal of last week's mood, he's become very attentive, even brought me a cup of tea in bed this morning! Things are definitely looking up.

Monday 22nd September

Grundy barbecue yesterday was, no surprises, a monumental booze-up. Lynda reportedly refused to set foot in the field but stood at the gate berating Mike Tucker about something, while Alan, apparently, has proposed to her that they joint-produce the Mystery Plays for the Christmas Show – definitely going where angels fear to tread, though he may not yet realise that. At least he'll be on the spot by then: Darrington vicarage has got to be underpinned so he and Amy are moving to Ambridge – in an extraordinary twist, into what used to be the surgery but which has now been converted back into a house and which, of course, was our vicarage until Robin Stokes left! Alice thrilled to think Amy will be just down the road: Amy thrilled as she will now get on school bus at same stop as Chris Carter, on whom she has developed a crush – though I'm not supposed to know that, Alice has sworn me to secrecy.

Ruth rang to say beef I'd ordered ready for collection. I mentioned Brian was putting a lot of time into thinking through future of farm at present and how positive he seemed: she seemed a bit surprised, said when he'd talked to David about it at the weekend, David had got the impression Brian was rather fed up at thought of yet another raft of CAP reforms, as if he hadn't got the stomach for it any more. Told her David must have got the wrong idea! Doesn't sound like the Brian I know – he's always up for a challenge.

Tuesday 23rd September

11 p.m. Finally found the right moment – Brian comfy with whisky in hand – to bring up my holiday plan. Started by apologising about the trust funds, but Brian brushed it away, said it was all forgotten, so, reassured, I launched into my idea about South Africa. Have to say Brian not as immediately enthusiastic as I'd hoped: thought he'd be thrilled by surprise element, and see specialness of it all, planning that had gone into it, etc. Instead he gave somewhat cautious response, said he'd have to think about it – well, his actual words were that he'd got 'rather a lot on' and didn't want to make any big decisions. Couldn't help feeling a bit let down: had so expected big hug, grateful thanks, and rest of evening looking through brochures, planning itinerary, choosing hotel, and tomorrow writing grovelling letter getting Alice off school, phoning Debbie and Kate… But in the end he did, at least, promise to give it some serious thought. So all in all… I think it's going to be all right. We'll get our holiday. But more than that, I think we've weathered the storm: not just about the trust funds, but everything that the past nine months has been about. Feel should sleep well tonight.

wednesday 24th september

Alice has invited six to sleep over on Saturday: shouldn't be surprised if Brian decamps elsewhere! Forecast still non-committal so spent morning making hamburgers (if fine), pizzas (if wet) and looking up cake recipes. Feel very fortunate not to be involved with F and P show this year: mum's agonising about her roses vs. Jill's and Lynda's (secret ingredient: llama beans!), Alistair's producing the most disgusting cakes which Shula and Daniel have to sample and this unusual marmalade thing has been taken to extremes. Rumour has it that Freda Fry's doing one with nettles, and even Jill's been experimenting (and not that successfully, I gather) with lime and passion fruit.

Brian's just announced he'll be out this evening: asked him if he had to be, as he's so tired: denied he was tired at all, said was I writing him off? Refuted this, instead emphasised how much he'll need a holiday by November. Was a bit snappy, said he's promised to think about it, he's told me he can't give me an answer straight away, can I please leave it for now. Oops.

Thursday 25th September

Am sure Brookfield, indeed every farm, has its moments of crisis, but equally sure can be nothing like here, where there always seems to be something! Decided last night that best thing I can do while Brian seems under so much pressure is to be supportive wife – hot meals, slippers warming by fire, etc. (well, not literally). So this evening had planned lovely supper – casserole of Tom's pork, delicious – and got hold of some organic wine recommended by Jack to have with it. Doesn't seem overly-ambitious, does it? But no. About seven got panic call from Adam – poor love, racing to get a field finished before dark, had misjudged the corner as he rounded the headland and ended up bashing the wretched great cultivator drill into a pylon. Thank God he wasn't hurt, but Brian had to rush straight out and look at it – not back in till after nine, and soaked through, as heavens had opened the second he got out to the field. Seems the drill won't be fixable on the farm, will have to go for engineering work – cost, a couple of thousand probably. Poor Brian seemed really fed up: one of those 'look what happens when I take my eye off the ball' moments – but thankfully seemed to perk up after glass of wine. Than I went and put out warm towels for him, he had a nice hot shower, and had his supper on a tray while we watched a wildlife documentary with Alice. So in the end it was a lovely, cosy, family evening. Which is the only consolation really, when things go wrong.

Friday 26th September

Brian out for the afternoon so good chance to get all my chores done so that we can concentrate on Alice this weekend. Once she'd gone off to school, wrapped her presents: feel sure new phone will be a success. Thought Brian would have kicked up a fuss, saying she runs up vast enough bill already, but he was surprisingly indulgent. Think he must be feeling as much as I do the fact that our baby is growing up.

Before he left, told him I'd ring round for quotes about getting cultivator drill fixed and that I saw it as my role to take as many of these tedious day-to-day worries off his shoulders as I could. He gave me his very lovely smile and a hug, said he didn't know what he'd have been without me. He can be quite sentimental sometimes.

Got to go to stables later to pay Alice's fee account and hoping for good long gossip with Shula, so quickly rang Lynda about the website: she confessed that the reason she took Mike on one side at the Grundys barbecue was because she thought he was Foursquare! Seems Foursquare's address is 'miketuckermilk' so Lynda not unreasonably thought it was Mike who was posting. Mike however strenuously denied this, says he is complete Luddite with computers, doesn't touch them unless he has to and was most insulted that Lynda thought it could be him in first place! So it now seems that Foursquare has cunningly been hiding behind not one, but two aliases – or, as Lynda put it, is a riddle wrapped inside a conundrum inside an enigma, or whatever the correct quote is.

Asked her what she proposes to do now, but she confesses she's stumped. Told her my Derek Fletcher theory but she says categorically it's not him, he far prefers to make his feelings known to one's face, which I agree is the flaw in my argument. She also gave me convincing reasons why it could not be any of the other supposed contenders, e.g. Mr Buttoned-Up from Glebelands. If trail has come to full stop, suppose we must leave it there. As I said to Lynda, there are some things in life which one will simply never know. And maybe sometimes it's better that way.

RESTITUTION

Sunday 28th September

6 p.m. Worst 48 hours of my life – and that includes last Christmas.

Friday, Brian had an accident, a car accident. A bad one. Head injury, broken ribs, punctured lung. Felpersham ICU: ventilator, drips, tubes. Never been so frightened in all my life. Never. Unconscious all weekend, only came round – thank god – thank god – this afternoon. Never been so grateful. All weekend, only one thought in my head: don't die. Don't die. I love you. I need you.

If I'd lost him – after everything – I love him so much.

Monday 29th September

7 a.m. Poor, poor Alice, what a birthday (15 today). She came home last night, had been with Pat and Tony all weekend, Mum at hospital with me, Adam keeping farm going.

229

Thought might finally sleep last night but very restless, so much going through my mind. Not tired though. Feel wired, hyper. Adrenalin, I suppose. Got to be strong for Brian, me, everyone. Keep self going.

Everyone's been wonderful. Wonderful. Couldn't think straight on Friday. When I got back and there was this police car in the yard, and this sweet pair of police constables, a man and a woman – well, a boy and a girl, really, asking if I was Mrs Aldridge... Everything flashes through your mind. It could have been anyone – Brian, Adam, Alice – even Kate or Debbie. In fact, Brian was the last person I thought of – he's always seemed so strong. Impregnable.

Made them tell me there and then in the yard, couldn't faff about going inside. Said I must get to hospital. They asked me if I needed driving there. Couldn't think. Had to think: Adam, out on farm: Alice, back from school any minute. Relatives who could look after her, they asked. Brain, paralysed, back into life. Then to Felpersham in police car, lights flashing, other-worldly, not happening to me.

Waiting, waiting, while they did tests, X-Rays, scans. Adam came. Stayed at hospital that night, all Saturday, Saturday night, too. No one seemed to know circumstances of crash: some woman dialled 999 – passer by? No one knows. She'd gone when the ambulance arrived. Did he black out at the wheel? Recurrence of epilepsy? God, I hope not. They can't yet say for sure.

Can hear Alice up and about. She's said she won't go to school – wants to see her dad.

9 a.m. Rang hospital: Brian 'stable'. Can't relax yet – still got chest drains in for fear of lung collapsing, and any head injury always a danger – but at least he's conscious. Any longer and – won't think about it. Not helpful.

Have devised plan of action: Adam coming in with me this morning: Mum'll bring Alice in this afternoon. Alice refusing to open any of her presents: will only do so with Brian. Told her she can phone Debbie and Kate for me: they want daily update. Also all village has been ringing: Jill, Chris, finding out through Mum, and Elizabeth, Oliver, Lynda, even, have left messages on machine. No time to ring back.

Just want to see Brian, be with him, hold him, make him better, will him better.

5 p.m. Just back from hospital. Alice in tears in car – horrible for her to see Brian like that – but better, she says, than not seeing him at all. Took along a couple of her presents but only to speculate about contents – has now decided to save them all to open when he comes home. Hoping to get her back to school tomorrow: one less person to think about.

Brian seemed agitated, keeps asking me about circumstances of the accident. Desperate to know if anyone else was involved, did he hit anyone? Told him skid marks seem to show he lost control of car. Told him no other vehicle at the scene, explained as yesterday – think he forgets – about mystery woman who, I'm sure, saved his life. Calmed for a second, then started going on about having to see David. Told him, as we had this morning, that farm was fine, Adam coping heroically, but didn't seem to soothe him. He's in pain, exhausted, he's got to stop worrying. Stupid though, you don't. Can't.

231

Jennifer's Diary

Tuesday 30th September

9.30 a.m. Kate's birthday today, she'll be 26.

Persuaded Alice to go back to school – think she'll be better off occupied. Also her friends are so concerned, all crowded round when I dropped her off, wanting to make fuss of her, etc. (Amy's been texting like mad, bless her). Going to phone Kate for her birthday, then into hospital. They were talking about moving Brian out of ICU today. Has to be good news.

4 p.m. Good job they'd warned me about moving Brian: when got to ICU his bed was empty! Now in private room, much better – phone, radio, TV, etc. Also own pyjamas! Brian just happy to be out of ICU. In flash of old self, says was doubly uneasy there as bed near the door always bad news.

Can't believe how fast they push you on in hospital these days – when you think that four days ago we didn't know if he'd live or die… Feel sick thinking about it.

Brian much better colour today but still going on about having to speak to David. Told him cultivator was mended and Adam had made up lost time, but not sure he believed me. Suppose he's just lying there going over and over things. Perhaps it'd be best if David did go and see him and they talked about the farm: for some reason Adam or me telling him just isn't the same! Felt flicker of exasperation – he can be so stubborn – but at same time absolute, flooding love. These signs of his 'usual self' just make me realise how much I love him. What a desperate case – even love his faults.

232

Had little chat with Mum while they changed some dressings – went out in hospital garden, rather nice, proper planting, Michaelmas daisies and beautiful rowan tree, not the usual sensible but soulless potentilla and chipped bark. She said how I was amazing her, being so strong – immediately wanted to collapse, of course – I'm all right as long as no one's kind to me, it just makes me want to break down. Told her I had to be, am only being strong for Brian. And how really feel, if didn't realise it before, all this year, that the accident's got 'second chance' written all over it in letters a foot high. And how determined I am to make the most of that chance.

Feeling slightly more up, though, now Brian's at least in his own room, and consultant cautiously optimistic, though of course they never commit themselves totally. They're talking about letting him go to loo by himself tomorrow – 'Big deal' says Brian – and wash himself and everything. Seems very tough regime, but Brian says it's to stop him getting institutionalised. They'll be lucky – he's probably plotting his escape even now!

9 p.m. When got back to hospital this evening, David just leaving – thank goodness. Perhaps Brian will stop worrying now. He seemed reassured, anyway.

Helped him change pyjama top, brush teeth, pinned up some of his cards. Told him how many people had been phoning, asking after him. Family still being terrific, Mum, Jack, Phil, Jill, Shula, of course, Pat, Tony. Lilian has sent shopful of flowers. Told him it showed how much people care. He gave a little smile – the family 'circling the wagons', he calls it. Cynic. But am sure he's secretly pleased.

233

wednesday 1st october

11 a.m. Brian described as having had 'comfortable' night – better in own room, ICU weirdly hushed yet so noisy, always machines beeping or nurse coming to check a drip/drain/whatever.

Got back from taking Alice to school to find Joe Grundy in yard on mission to 'borrow' a few ewes to run in his field to impress the Planning Inspector over the pole barn appeal – can that still really be going on? Another world. Luckily David here, refused on our behalf. Managed to get rid of Joe fairly quickly, though he was muttering something about Brian doubtless being fed up of 'women's prattle' by now – hope he doesn't take it into his head to go and visit him! Brian won't thank me!

David stopped for a chat – had come to offer help to Adam, if needed – and could feel my eyes filling up. There's something about David that's so reassuring, so solid, so virtuous, if that's not the wrong word – this silly badger thing notwithstanding – that just made me want to flop into his arms and dissolve. When I tried to thank him for all he was doing he seemed really embarrassed, wouldn't have it at all – instead touchingly assured me he was committed to doing everything he could for all of us, would go on doing it, whatever, and that I could trust him completely. Honestly had to bite my lip. In moments like this there's so much of Phil – and of Grandad – about him. A really good man.

Must have been the conversation with David, because after he'd gone, came inside, put kettle on, sat down at table and then suddenly folded in on myself, sobbing my heart out. Suppose just haven't been able to let go – not in front of Brian, Alice, not even Mum or Adam. Always 'one day at a time', positive, upbeat – exhausting, and not what I really felt/feel at all. Terror, palpitations, almost, the churning stomach, never knowing what I was going to find at the hospital, and, that first weekend, scared to leave him, even to go to the loo, for fear of what I might be coming back to. The great void that would be life without him – and me, just nothing, reduced to nothing.

Inconceivable to think that I ever, even for a moment, at Christmas, thought I could leave him or live without him. I wasn't thinking straight, of course, but also I wasn't dealing with the Brian I knew, or the me I know, come to that. He'd hurt me so badly that I thought he'd destroyed a part of me I might not get back – a part of us we might not get back – and maybe I thought the only way forward was to destroy the rest. But I didn't feel like that for long and I don't think I ever really believed it – it never really rang true. And if I ever did doubt our ability to get over it, the way I've felt the last few days has shown me, that for me at least, I love him just as much as I ever did, if not more, because of all we've been through. And I so, so just want him home so I can look after him, love him, and be a wife again, whole-heartedly.

I had so much to smile about in the early days of my marriage. And I hope I will have again.

5 p.m. Feel a bit better having seen Brian: chest drain coming out tomorrow – and they've taken away his fluid drip and morphine. Just on paracetamol now – incredible how far he's come in a few days. Sitting up OK, but moving up the bed obviously painful, even talking sometimes. But clearly relieved that by tomorrow he won't look quite so much like something from horror film, as he puts it.

Also very sweetly thinking of me – so lovely given way I was feeling this morning – says I'm wearing myself out racing to and from Felpersham. Suggested I have a break tomorrow, come in for the evening, but do farmers market in Borchester in the day for complete change of scene. Initially not keen, then realised really ought to do market or we'll get all out of sync. with the venison – maybe Mum could help. Anyway, eventually agreed: perhaps a day without visitors would do Brian good too, and if I go in the evening Alice and Adam can come as well. Eventually settled on this.

So I have sort of day off tomorrow – which in a sense will be a relief. Strange though – have spent entire week talking, thinking about nothing but Brian – not sure if capable of processing any other thoughts, has been so all-consuming. Told him I'd be still be thinking about him, and will phone: he smiled, said he didn't deserve me. Told him I loved him. Desperate to give him proper hug. And have one back.

Thursday 2nd October

7 p.m. As arrived at hospital late afternoon, bumped into Tony – last person I was expecting to see – and he reported that who should have been with Brian when he got there but Joe Grundy! And Ruth and David, apparently, before him – so much for poor Brian's visitor-free day! Brian obviously feeling the strain, as once Joe had gone he'd sent Tony off to the WRVS tea bar while he closed his eyes for a bit. Joe, apparently, had eaten best part of a pound of grapes – Tony very miffed as only stalks left – and had been boring Brian rigid about the pole barn! Tony reckoned he'd probably set Brian's recovery back by about a week.

Hung around and had cup of tea with Tony, who said he'd push off as we were there – then went up dreading what state Brian'd be in – any visitors exhausting, let alone Joe. He was obviously tired and a bit, I don't know, subdued at first, but as time went on, somehow better in himself. Calmer.

Pleased to hear from Adam about finishing the Brookfield drilling but when Alice started prattling on about Justin Timberlake could see he was drifting off, so we didn't stay too long. Adam teased him about missing Harvest Home tomorrow – 'some people will go to any lengths,' etc – and Brian's eyes filled with tears. Says he just wants to be home again, home safe with us all.

That's all I want, too.

Friday 3rd October

8 p.m. Almost too tired to write but as consultant says that, all being well, Brian can come home after the weekend I know I shan't have a moment after that!

It was after the consultant told us – suppose it's not surprising really, I'd been so determined to be strong for Brian, was bound to crack sooner or later. There's such a lot of rubbish talked about who's the strong one in any relationship, whereas anyone knows it's entirely variable – you're strong for each other according to circumstances. And it's so often deceptive, with the outwardly 'weaker' one the real ballast of the whole thing – just look at Robert and Lynda! I've spent most of the last nine months trying to analyse where the power balance lies between me and Brian – and look what a see-saw that's been. All I keep coming back to is that we complement each other. Sometimes he's the strong one and sometimes it's me.

Anyway, my being strong completely fell apart today. After the consultant had gone, Brian, to hide his own relief I know, made some quip about Lilian only sending so many flowers so she wouldn't have had to send a wreath. Typical Brian, cover up the real feeling with a joke. But for me… the sheer release of hearing he could come home after so much tension…

When I think about this time last week – those injuries, and imagining never having him home, never holding him again, never again hearing one of his little jokes… well, all my composure simply avalanched away. Found myself sobbing, just like the other morning, telling him about how Friday was for me, coming home to find the police in the yard, and the fear through all last weekend, the thought of losing him, never having the chance to show him how much I loved and wanted him, to look after him, care for him, just to be with him. At same time so cross with myself, had been so determined not to break down in front of him, but couldn't help it. And he just held out his arms – as best he could, poor love – and I crept in, trying not to hurt him, and kissed him, properly, and told him how much I loved him. 'I love you too, Jenny,' he said. 'With all my heart.'

This has been the most traumatic nine months ever. God knows, I've had some turmoil in my life, but nothing compared to this.

It's so odd when I think about me, Tony and Lilian growing up. I always thought she'd be the one with the dramatic life, but instead I've been the one at the thick of it, while Tony, bless him, seems to be destined to stay in the background, quietly calving a heifer or planting his leeks. I'll never know the answers to any of the questions I asked myself earlier this year – whether I'd have been better off as a single parent, or if I'd stayed with Roger – and I'm going to stop asking them. From now on, I'm going to deal with the here and now, which means Brian, and the children, and the farm. Siobhan is gone, over, and as far as I'm concerned, forgotten. If the past year's achieved anything, it's made me be a bit more truthful about myself and about me and Brian, made me realise what real love is, and honesty, and trust.

But what it's shown me most of all is that things happen; life unfolds. All you can determine is how much mess you create along the way. And sometimes even that's beyond your control.